Alternative math Techniques

When nothing else seems to work.

Now you've got it! :)

Subtraction
Eliminating Borrowing

...liminate borrowing. Then solve the problem.

$$54 + 4$$
$$-26 + 4$$

$$58$$
$$-30$$

$$54 + 4$$
$$-30$$

$$58$$
$$-30$$
$$\overline{38}$$

$$54$$
$$-26$$

$$54$$
$$-26 + 4$$

$$48 - 1$$
$$-29 + 1 \quad -30$$

OK

$$49$$
$$-30$$

$$48$$
$$-29 + 1$$

$$48$$
$$-29$$
$$\overline{(19)}$$

$$+ 3 \quad 85$$
$$7 + 3 \quad -70$$

$$82 \quad 82 + 3 \quad 85$$
$$-67 + 3 \quad -70 \quad -70$$
$$\overline{15}$$

$$54$$
$$-10$$
$$\overline{(44)}$$

OK

OK

$$86 \quad 81$$
$$-80 \quad -75 + 5$$
$$\overline{(6)} \quad -80 + 5$$
$$81 + 5$$
$$-80$$

$$52$$
$$-8$$

$$+2$$

$$25$$

$$29$$

$$32$$
$$-13 + 7$$

Richard Cooper

SOPRIS WEST

Editing by Francelia Sevin
Text layout and design by Dianne Gorman
Cover design by Dianne Gorman

Published and Distributed by

SOPRIS
WEST
EDUCATIONAL SERVICES

4093 Specialty Place • Longmont, Colorado 80504 • (303) 651–2829
www.sopriswest.com

239ALTMATH/4-04/BAN/1.5M/357

Dedication

This book is dedicated to all the students who came to me for help with math. I thank them for helping me learn how to teach them.

About the Author

Richard Cooper, Ph.D., is the founder and director of the Center for Alternative Learning, an organization dedicated to providing educational and social support to children and adults with learning disabilities, problems, and differences. He earned his doctorate in education at the University of Pittsburgh (PA) in 1978 and his master's degree in counseling at the InterAmerican University in Puerto Rico.

Dr. Cooper develops teaching methods and instructional tools for individuals who learn differently and maintains a private practice through which he provides assessment, counseling, and tutoring for children and adults. Dr. Cooper is also an internationally recognized speaker and instructor. He was a member of the observer delegation from the United States to the 1997 UNESCO Conference on Adult Education in Hamburg, Germany, and presented "Using Alternative Math Techniques with Dyslexics" at the International Dyslexia Conference in Uppsala, Sweden, in 2002. In addition, Dr. Cooper is a founding member and past president of the National Association for Adults with Special Learning Needs.

Contents

Chapter 3: Helping Students Learn Number Facts

Chapter 4: Teaching Basic Math Concepts

Chapter 8: Teaching Division

Chapter 9: Teaching Fractions, Decimals, and Percentages

Conclusion

Bibliography

Preface

This eclectic collection of instructional concepts, techniques, and tips is based on my own experiences learning math as a student with a learning problem as well as on my more than 20 years of clinical experience as a learning specialist working with students and adults who struggle with math. The techniques presented are the ones I have found most effective in my own classroom. Many of them relate to the thought processes that interfere with the learning of all subjects, not just math. These alternative techniques will help you teach students who are not learning in the same way as other students. Along with each technique is an explanation as to why students may not grasp a concept or remember an operation.

This is neither a comprehensive book about teaching math to students with special needs, nor a curriculum that covers all of the concepts of arithmetic. It also does not detail the common techniques for teaching math skills (such as the use of manipulatives, problem-solving skills, or real-life situations). Rather, this book presents alternatives to common methods, suggesting what to do when students are not successful.

The instructional concepts and techniques that follow are helpful not only for teaching students with special learning needs but also for students who exhibit poor math skills for a variety of reasons. Some students may be developmentally behind and not ready to master concepts and operations. Other students may have undiagnosed learning problems or problems that are narrow in scope, limiting only certain aspects of their acquisition of skills. Still others may have learning problems that are not severe and so are not formally diagnosed. Students in all of these groups often exhibit similar thought processes to a greater or lesser degree. By increasing your awareness of the behavioral manifestations of learning differences, you can find the instructional techniques that work best with your particular students.

I have found that the same problems that can limit the acquisition of language skills (reading, writing, and spelling) can also limit the acquisition of math skills. Because I work with both children and adults, the techniques I've presented are cross-generational. I've used them successfully with all ages. The child who does not learn the difference between odd and even numbers grows up to be the adult who does not know the difference between odd and even numbers. The child who does not learn how to measure grows up to be the adult who struggles with measurements. The child who does not master the number facts becomes the adult who does not know the number facts, and on and on. So, whether you are working with children or adults does not matter. These techniques will help them understand and apply mathematical concepts and operations.

Introduction

This collection of alternative techniques for teaching arithmetic operations and math concepts will help you instruct students who struggle with math. Not every technique is necessary for every student, but the more ways you have to help students understand concepts and manipulate numbers, the more likely they are to remember the concepts and to be able to solve math problems. A number of principles underlie the concepts and techniques offered in this book. These principles, based on my own experience working with students, apply to students of all ages who struggle with math.

They include:

- Math does not come naturally to everyone.

- A person who sequences (counts) rather than groups numbers will have difficulty learning math.

- Individuals who do not pay attention to numbers and quantitative concepts in their environments find learning math similar to learning a foreign language. It is difficult for them to learn math because: 1) like a foreign language, the terms are unfamiliar; and 2) they do not use quantitative concepts and numbers in their everyday thoughts.

- Informational gaps limit a student's ability to make progress in math. Students who have gaps in their understanding of math are often unable to learn higher-level operations and concepts because they do not know a lower-level concept or do not possess a lower-level skill. The most obvious example is long division. Students who do not know all the multiplication facts cannot master division.

- Quantitative concepts are represented by math vocabulary. Students who do not know the meaning of math terms have difficulty understanding quantitative concepts.

- "If you don't use it, you lose it." This cliché applies to the learning of math. Students who do not use the math skills they learn will, over time, forget them.

In my work I often find that students have weak math skills because of learning problems.
These students:

- Have perceptual, processing, and/or communication difficulties.

- Need far more repetition than other students.

- Benefit from alternative techniques so much so that alternative techniques often mean the difference between success and failure.

- Will make more mistakes in computations than others; therefore, they need to get into the habit of checking their calculations.

- Have perceptual, processing, and/or communication differences that are exacerbated by stress, anxiety, time pressure, performance pressure, fatigue, and embarrassment. Students make more errors under these conditions.

On a Personal Note:

Throughout this book I've included anecdotes of my experiences working with students. The names have been changed, but the situations are real. These anecdotes illustrate problems you may encounter in your own classroom and also provide possible solutions.

Getting at the Root of Math Problems

When trying to help math students who are not "getting it," it is often helpful to consider the underlying factors that contribute to their difficulties. Sometimes teachers assume that the symptoms of a math problem are the root of the problem, which can lead to instructional approaches that are not effective. So, it's important to clarify the difference between symptoms and roots.

Symptoms of Math Problems

Math learning problems are varied and complex and are not the same for every student. The *symptoms* of math learning problems, however, can be grouped into three categories:

1. Computation errors

2. Weak quantitative concepts

3. Poor performance in daily math activities.

Computation errors are particularly frustrating for students because they seem like inexplicable errors that result in poor grades. Imagine the frustration when a student makes an error like *5 + 5 = 11* or *17 – 8 = 10*. Complex math operations are solved using computations that rely on basic number facts. A student may have most of the facts correct and yet make one error on one number fact, resulting in an incorrect answer.

Weak quantitative concepts compound the problems caused by computation errors. Students who do not understand the concept of division may reverse numbers and divide by the wrong number. For example when asked, "What is 23 divided by 42?" students may write: $23 \overline{)42}$

Likewise, when students believe that the word *double* simply means *more* rather than *twice* as much, or that % means *less* or *on sale*, they are left feeling that math does not make sense.

Poor performance in everyday math (such as counting money, making change, telling time, or measuring) is the source of much frustration. For example, to find out how many chairs are in a room, students may have to count the chairs because they cannot multiply the number of rows by the number of chairs in a row. Or, when purchasing an item, students may pay with a bill rather than coins because they want to avoid being embarrassed by paying the wrong amount in coins.

These three symptoms of math learning problems are observed in students of all ages and abilities. For students of normal intellectual ability, these symptoms are often compounded by **avoidance** and **math anxiety**. Some students try their best to avoid math, and others have a true sense of anxiety about anything related to computations or quantitative concepts.

Avoidance. It is part of human nature to avoid what you do not like or do not understand. Avoidance behavior is often a defense mechanism students use to shield themselves from situations that are potentially frustrating or embarrassing. For example, students who need much more time than others to complete math homework may forget to bring home their math books. In this way, they avoid the frustration of doing math homework. Or, when playing a game that uses dice, they may let others tell them how many moves to make rather than adding the dots on the dice themselves. Avoidance patterns, like other habits, grow slowly over time and can have long-lasting effects on behavior.

Math anxiety. In an inservice course I teach each year on using alternative math techniques, teachers of kindergarten and the primary grades report that, in general, students not only like math but are also excited about learning math. Teachers of higher grades report that a significant portion of students dislike math and even exhibit math anxiety. The same observations are commonly reported by parents. Children are not born with math anxiety. It develops over time, usually as the result of frustration and/or failure.

Roots of Math Problems

Although computation errors, weak quantitative concepts, and poor math performance are exacerbated by avoidance and math anxiety, the true roots of math problems are:

1. Information gaps

2. Insufficient or ineffective instruction

3. Learning differences, difficulties, or disabilities.

Information gaps. We all have gaps in our knowledge. This is particularly true today in this information age. However, the information gaps of the students we are concerned with are not gaps in new information, but rather gaps in information about math concepts and operations. Students may have learned and forgotten the information or may never have learned the information because, although the information was presented, they did not understand it. Some students need more practice than others. Without sufficient intensity, the skills are lost. For example, students who never fully understand fractions may be able to deal with halves and quarters in everyday situations, but other fractions (e.g., *three-fifths*) and the numbers that represent them are meaningless.

Insufficient or ineffective instruction. Students who suffer from math anxiety, manifest avoidance behavior, or have information gaps often have not received sufficient and effective instruction. These students may need to be taught differently and given more, repeated practice.

Remediation

Josh spent three years of high school learning math from one teacher who only used worksheets. The school district had set up a remedial classroom to serve students who had weak math skills, and Josh was participating in it. The students worked on Number Fact worksheets every day. Once a month they were given timed tests. Students who passed the timed tests were moved into general education math classes. Those who did not pass remained in the remedial class. Since Josh counted on his fingers to do computations, he never was able to pass the timed test. He remained in the remedial classroom, completing worksheets until he graduated from high school. Josh needed to be taught using alternative techniques, not drill and practice in the same way over and over.

Learning differences, difficulties, and disabilities. The severity of learning problems varies. Not every student who has a learning problem has a severe one or one that is disabling. Learning differences are on a continuum. Students who have **learning disabilities** have significant challenges acquiring basic academic skills. Students who have **learning difficulties** exhibit the same thought processes as those with learning disabilities, have the same behaviors, and make the same types of mistakes—but to a lesser extent and less frequently. Students who have **learning differences** also exhibit the same thought processes, have the same behaviors, and make the same types of mistakes—but to a lesser extent and less frequently than those with learning difficulties. *Figure 1.1* depicts the commonality of the students whose learning can be described by these three terms. We can refer to students in all three of these "categories" as learning differently, thereby reducing the negative effect of labeling.

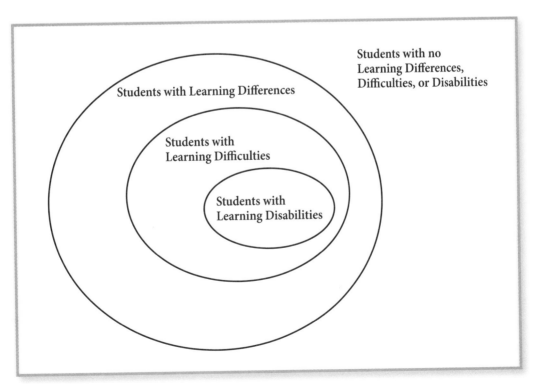

Fig 1.1: The relationship between learning differences, difficulties, and disabilities.

In the classroom I have observed many learning differences, difficulties, and disabilities that interfere with students' mastery of math skills, including problems with:

- Tactile and motor movement perception and processing (which cause poor handwriting and motor coordination).

- Visual perception and processing (which cause poor visual organization and difficulty interpreting visual stimulation).

- Right/left discrimination (which causes confusion between items that have either/or relationships). Problems in this area may affect spatial relations, language, and/or quantity—all three of which are involved in the learning and understanding of math.

- Racing mind (which causes quick processing and communicating of information that often misses details or causes errors).

- Memory (which causes incorrect or incomplete storage and retrieval of information).

- Organization (which interferes with grouping ideas, thoughts, and experiences).

- Sequencing (which interferes with the proper ordering of events in time and objects in space).

- Auditory perception and processing (which often results in an underdeveloped vocabulary).

- Reading problems (which cause inaccurate reading of directions, word problems, and textbooks, limiting independent learning).

A Postscript About Labels

The terminology in this book is different from the terminology usually associated with special learning needs. Labels such as dyslexia, dyscalculia, dysgraphia, ADD, and ADHD (and many other labels) are often misunderstood. They also often mean different things to different people. Focusing on the behavioral manifestation of thought processes rather than on labels will help you grasp alternative ways of looking at students' problems learning math. This does not mean that the labels traditionally used to describe students who struggle in school are not useful or necessary. The use of nontraditional terms, however, leads to instructional approaches that encompass how students process information. The techniques in this book are matched to the thought processes of students who struggle learning math, not to labels.

Remediations, Adaptations, and Accommodations

Very often students who struggle with math (or who just think differently) need remediations, adaptations, or accommodations in order to learn quantitative concepts and perform mathematical operations.

Remediations are re-instruction in subject matter that either was not mastered by students when originally taught or was learned but then forgotten.

Adaptations are changes to materials or instruction that enable students to complete tasks or to learn things that would otherwise be difficult for them to master.

Accommodations are alternative methods and/or assistive devices that enable students to perform tasks that they would otherwise not be able to perform (due to disabilities). An accommodation is a legal right of a student with a documented disability.

In practice, what is an adaptation for one student may be an accommodation for another. Very often, remediations, adaptations, and accommodations are needed to enable students who struggle with math and/or who think differently to learn quantitative concepts and perform mathematical operations. This chapter provides remediations, adaptations, and accommodations you can use with students who have problems learning math. The suggestions are not comprehensive; they are aimed at helping those students whose specific learning differences are most frequently encountered in my own practice. Don't limit their use to one or two students in your classroom though. You may find that all your students benefit from some of these suggestions.

I have found that some learning difficulties interfere more with the learning of math than others. The following sections address specific trouble spots. Keep in mind that what helps one student with a problem may not help another student with the same problem. Some of the suggestions are simple; others are complex. For example, one simple adaptation is using colored paper for an activity. Over time, you may find that a student performs better when assignments are to be completed on a specific color of paper. It only takes a little more planning and time to adapt materials for this student. A more complex adaptation is to use colored pens or pencils or colored text to help a student understand information or stay organized. This adaptation takes more planning to implement than the colored paper adaptation, but older students may choose to take the extra time and effort to write in multiple colors because it works for them.

Many of the suggestions detailed in this chapter can be layered into your instruction. Begin with a small step, concept, or operation. Add more as students experience success.

Auditory Perception and Processing

Students who have auditory perception and processing problems often manifest underdeveloped vocabularies. When students don't hear words clearly, their language skills develop at a slower rate than their peers' skills. Words, especially abstract terms or terms that have double or multiple meanings, take longer for students to learn. Over time, this results in students having underdeveloped or ambiguous vocabularies. Auditory perception and processing problems affect oral communication, reading comprehension, and critical thinking skills. Students may not hear the difference between *numerator* and *denominator* but only hear the suffix *-ator*. Or they may not hear /*ths*/ at the end of the decimal or fraction numbers, e.g., *tenths* and *eighths*.

Remediations

Students who have auditory problems need to increase and sharpen their vocabularies. In addition to providing them with systematic and regular study of words and their meanings, try the following remediations.

- ▶ Teach students the structure of language (parts of speech, prefixes, suffixes, root words, etc.) and how to use context clues. Understanding structure increases students' ability to understand language when they don't hear clearly.

- ▶ Provide students with audiotapes of the math terms that they need to know, with the sounds of the words pronounced clearly. Audiotapes can help them improve their listening skills and become comfortable with vocabulary.

Adaptations and Accommodations

Visual cues are important for students with auditory problems, so make them a regular part of your instruction. Try the following ideas.

- ▶ Provide written material with illustrations to supplement oral instruction.

- ▶ Adapt worksheets and tests by providing a glossary of key words that students can refer to.

- ▶ Give students extra time to complete assignments and tests. Underdeveloped vocabularies reduce reading speed, so students need to be accommodated.

Handwriting

Although fine-motor-control problems affect fewer students than other problems, poor handwriting resulting from poor motor control does interfere with the development of math skills. Besides being frustrated, students who are unable to read the numbers they have just written will have difficulty checking their work. Students with poor handwriting have to rely on memory to determine what they wrote, and they often cannot remember the numbers.

Remediations

Criticizing students' poor handwriting or expecting students to improve on their own is not an effective way of addressing handwriting problems. Present handwriting exercises in a positive manner so that students understand that the exercises are meant to help them improve a skill, not to punish them for sloppy handwriting.

▶ Doodling can improve fine motor control. Encourage students to begin by drawing large shapes, figures, and designs of their choosing. Then have them reduce the size of their doodles gradually, giving their fine motor skills a work out.

▶ Penmanship exercises also improve handwriting.

Adaptations and Accommodations

Sometimes just having extra time is all that a student needs in order to write more legibly and check answers. Assistive devices, developed for students with physical disabilities, can also help students with poor motor control.

▶ Assistive devices include grips, guides, and paper with raised lines.

▶ Simply using a different kind of pen or pencil can help students improve their handwriting. Encourage students to experiment with various types of pencils and pens. Try felt-tip pens, pens with erasable ink, and varied pen thicknesses.

▶ Show students how to use paper more effectively to improve their handwriting. Have them stabilize their papers with frames or adhesives. That way, they can focus on legibly writing numbers instead of on holding down their papers.

▶ Purchase or create graph paper that is sized to students' specific handwriting. The extra lines provide a visual guide that makes it easier to format numbers and mathematical symbols.

▶ Simply having students turn their lined papers sideways can help them to write more legibly because they can use the vertical lines as a guide.

On a Personal Note:

Graph Paper

After completing school, many professionals, including accountants and engineers, use graph paper when they work with numbers. Yet in schools in the United States, graph paper is often only used for specific math procedures such as graphing. In some countries, math students of all levels use notebooks that have both vertical and horizontal lines. My wife, Anne-Louise, who grew up in Sweden, tells me that her math notebooks were always comprised of graph paper.

If you have all of your students use graph paper for all of their math assignments as a matter of course, then those students who need the extra lines will not feel different or inadequate. All of your students, even those with significant visual organization or motor difficulties, will be able to correctly line up math problems and keep their work organized..

Limitations in short-term, long-term, and working memory significantly impact the ability to learn math. Sometimes difficulties appear as memory problems but are really other problems (such as a racing mind, right/left discrimination difficulty, or poor study skills). Before you assume that a student just cannot remember things, try the techniques that follow. If they ameliorate the memory problem, the student will develop a sense of self-confidence and the knowledge that there are specific techniques to use for learning and remembering.

Remediations

One reason students have difficulty remembering is that they have not practiced the tasks or studied the material long enough. By increasing the number of repetitions or the length of time of study, you can help students remember. Teach students mnemonic clues (e.g., acronyms, memory pegs, sequences, strategies, and visualizations) for things they find difficult to remember.

- ▶ Increase repetition by linking learning to common activities. For example, every time students walk up a set of steps, have them recall their multiplication facts.

- ▶ Assist students who have good visual memories by putting information into concept maps, visual organizers, or frameworks. For students with good auditory memories, use acronyms, rhymes, and sayings to help them remember information.

- ▶ Teach students to use **memory pegs** and memory stacks to remember information that they need for quick and accurate computations. Memory pegs are words pegged to a set of numbers (e.g., *1/run, 2/zoo, 3/tree).* The words are associated with the information to be remembered. **Memory stacks** are a visualization of exaggerated pictures, stacked one upon another, that are associated with the information that needs to be remembered. For example, to help students remember the steps of division (divide, multiply, subtract, and bring down), you may suggest: "Visualize your **d**ad (**d**ivide) carrying your **m**other (**m**ultiply) on his shoulders, with your **s**ister (**s**ubtract) on your mother's shoulders, and your **b**rother (**b**ring down) jumping off your sister's shoulders."

- ▶ Mental rehearsal is a technique that many students already use when they want to remember something, such as a friend's phone number. They repeat the number over and over. Have students mentally rehearse math facts, concepts, and operations.

- ▶ Make information portable. Write information on index cards or study sheets so that students can easily review until they have mastered it.

Adaptations and Accommodations

If students are still not able to remember math facts, operations, formulas, or concepts after you've instructed them in memory techniques and tried alternative instructional techniques, then adapt their math assignments and tests. Try the following adaptations:

- ▶ Provide formulas or the steps for math operations on their worksheets and tests or on separate sheets of paper.

- ▶ Keep memory tools and visual cues, such as conversion charts, in plain sight so that students with memory challenges can complete tasks successfully.

▶ Provide calculators and other manipulatives, such as an abacus, to accommodate students with special needs (also see *Using Calculators* at the end of this chapter).

Organization

Many students, not just those who have learning problems, have difficulty organizing their things and/or their thoughts. Disorganization can cause mundane problems, like not being able to find a pencil, and significant problems, like not following a logical sequence when solving an equation.

Disorganization of things is obvious. You see students' messy worksheets, book bags, and desks. Disorganization of thoughts is less obvious. You do not see chaotic thoughts or illogical thinking, but there are cues that can tell you when students have disorganized thoughts.

Students who have organizational problems often have difficulty with categories and grouping. For example, it is difficult for them to understand the differences among the categories of fractions, mixed numbers, and improper fractions. And they may not understand groups, such as numbers in their place values, which may cause errors when estimating and rounding.

Remediations

Teach organization, do not expect it.

▶ Teach students to label their work: to write their names, the date, and page numbers on every assignment.

▶ Teach students to keep work organized so that as they complete assignments or tests they can find them later and do not become confused.

▶ Have students practice organizing. Set up organizational activities, with both things and with ideas, so that students develop organizational skills.

▶ Remind students to stay organized. Students who learn to structure their work and are reminded to use their skills eventually learn to be organized.

Adaptations and Accommodations

▶ When students need more than basic organizational skill practice, try adapting their math materials to help them organize.

▶ Lay out worksheets and tests with blank lines for students to label activities and provide designated spaces for each type of math operation.

▶ Color code your instructional materials. For example, use one color for new material and another for review activities.

▶ Plan to give students extra time to get organized and to stay organized.

Do you often find your mind flooded with so many thoughts about so many things that you become overwhelmed? Does your mind race off to visualize the first step in a series of directions so that you do not pay attention to the rest of the steps?

When screening for learning and attention differences, I always ask these two questions. Although everyone occasionally experiences these symptoms, students who frequently experience them probably have racing minds.

The term **racing mind** means thoughts that move so fast that students make errors of omission or respond in ways that indicate they've jumped to the next thought (also called *triggering*). Racing thoughts often result in students not paying attention to detail, acting on assumptions, and rushing through activities. Students who have racing thoughts usually do not check their work, or they check it so quickly that they miss even obvious errors.

On a Personal Note:

Terminology

I prefer the term "racing mind" to the terms Attention Deficit Disorder (ADD) and Attention Deficit Hyperactivity Disorder (ADHD). There are varying degrees of attention problems. Although the behaviors associated with severe attention problems cause significant difficulties, many students have milder symptoms and much less difficulty. By reserving the term ADD for the most serious problems, we free ourselves to treat milder attention problems differently.

The same thought patterns that challenge students in learning can interfere with their ability to function in other areas of life, including work and social interactions. Attention problems are often associated with behavioral problems. The racing-mind thought process that causes behavioral problems also causes information to be processed differently.

Rather than labeling students and having them see themselves as having a deficit or disorder, use the term "racing mind" so that they can better understand their own thoughts and behaviors. Students can then focus on the positive aspects. While the word "deficit" emphasizes the negative, "racing mind" emphasizes the positive. It implies different not defective. This positive perspective can make a significant difference in a student's self-image.

I often use the analogy of a raging river to help people understand the *racing mind*. Imagine a river, like the one in *Figure 2.1,* beginning as a trickle high in the mountains, increasing in volume as it flows down the mountains through the valleys, and across the plains, to the sea. When the river swells because of heavy rain, the water rages down the mountains, toward the sea, causing much destruction and chaos. However, if engineers build a number of hydroelectric dams on the river, the raging waters are not only controlled, but they also produce productive energy. By seeing the racing mind as a resource to be tapped, students learn to harness the power of their minds and avoid some of the chaos and destruction.

Figure 2.1: Racing mind is like a raging river.

Positive Aspects

There are many positive aspects of racing mind, including:

Quick wits. Although students can use their quick wits to be class clowns, they can also outsmart competitors in sports and avoid confrontations with bullies.

High energy. Students with high levels of energy can work and play faster and harder than others.

Taking risks. Students may go beyond the limits of what others are willing to do (which can be advantageous in competitions, sports, games, and even in business). Risk-takers often become entrepreneurs. Although people who strike out on their own sometimes fail, there is much to be said for people who break through barriers.

Tenacity. Hard work and tenacity often result in high productivity.

Problem-solving ability. Students may consider a myriad of possible solutions before others have even grasped the problem.

Adaptability. Creativity often accompanies a racing mind. Students may be masters of flexibility and substitution. They find ways to accomplish tasks with whatever is available.

Quick thinking and movements. Together, quick thinking and quick movements make for excellent athletic ability. Students may even become sports extremists like cliff skiers or skydivers.

Observance. Being observant is the positive side of being distractible. In many environments, individuals with racing minds excel.

Multitasking. High energy levels and quick thinking enable students to work on several projects simultaneously.

Negative Aspects

Not everything about a racing mind is positive. Its negative aspects can limit productivity, cause errors and confusion, and reduce self-confidence. If a student is attentive to too many things or is distracted, it is difficult to focus on the task at hand. Negative aspects of racing mind include:

Jumping ahead. When multiple steps of directions are given, students begin to visualize or plan the first step and do not process the rest of the directions.

Triggering. Students' thoughts overshoot, missing the correct response. Trigger errors include substituting a synonym for a word when reading aloud, using the wrong word when speaking, and making simple math mistakes. When adding a sequence of numbers, students make errors as they try to hold numbers in their heads. For example, when adding $8 + 7 + 9 + 7 + 8$, students think $8 + 7 = 15$, and jump to *16* before adding the next number. Another example of triggering occurred with my student Gelsomina, who, when asked "What is 5×5?," responded "*36*." When asked to try again, she responded "*25*, just like I said." She was unaware that she had jumped to the answer to 6×6.

Tangential thinking. Students go off on tangents in conversations, when solving problems, or when writing a paragraph. They may be talking about one topic when an idea triggers a thought about another topic, taking the conversation in a new direction. After a few triggers, the conversation is far afield, and no one knows what they are talking about. Another example is when students are trying to solve a word problem and start thinking about the color of the objects mentioned rather than focusing on the numbers.

Skipping. Students skip words as they write, steps in number sequences, and information in conversations without being aware of it.

Observance. It is good to be observant in some situations, but in others being too observant (or distractible) means that you are unable to effectively focus on the task at hand.

Excitability. Students envision end results or products and so do not complete the tasks to get there. They may take on or start too many projects but not complete them. Or they may collect many things, imagining all the possible uses of them.

Remediations

▶ Having a racing mind can be a gift or a curse, depending on whether students are able to control it for productive uses or let their thought process control them, causing chaos. In order to use their minds to their advantage, students need to develop self-awareness. The better students know themselves, the better they can channel and control their racing minds. Learning to appreciate their differences, instead of focusing on negatives, sets the stage for students to use their minds positively. The techniques that follow can help you empower students to channel their energy to succeed.

▶ Help students learn which things in the environment they can control to their benefit. Students who lack internal structure often resist external structure (imposed on them by others). They may spend much time and energy trying to evade or unravel structures. Accepting the fact that they need structure, and requesting help in establishing that structure, can make the difference between success and failure. When students learn to structure and plan for success, they are more likely to succeed. Students need to know whether they work better in uncluttered workspaces or busy ones, quiet places or places where some noise fills the void of silence. When students know how they work best, help them structure their environments to achieve their goals.

▶ Provide frames (heavy sheets of paper with windows cut in them) that students can use to isolate necessary information and parts of assignments. This simple tool helps them focus on the task at hand.

▶ A racing mind can create many errors, so students need to know when they are most likely to make errors and learn to check their work often. Teach students that stress, anxiety, time and performance pressures, and fatigue accelerate the racing mind, increasing the likelihood of errors. When students are aware, they can take more care.

▶ Show students how to use small looping circles to check their work (see *Figure 2.2*). With this technique, students loop back to check a few answers at a time instead of waiting until the end and checking all the answers. They learn to break tasks into small segments and check for accuracy. When they have finished one segment of a task, students loop back and check that each step in that segment is complete.

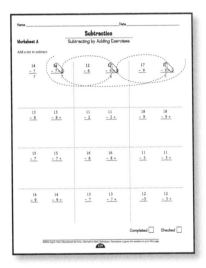

Figure 2.2: Students "draw" small looping circles with a finger to check their work as they complete a few problems at a time rather than waiting until they have completed them all.

▶ Teach students to stop and think before they act. This simple habit can eliminate some impulsive behaviors and their resulting errors. Although "stop and think" is simple, it is not necessarily easy. It is not enough for students to say they are going to stop and think; they must practice often. They also need help to learn this new behavior. Once learned, however, "stop and think" has far-reaching benefits.

▶ Help students relax. Students who seem "wired" often have difficulty using visualization and relaxation audiotapes. They need a more engaging experience that only a real person can provide. When students learn to visualize and look ahead, anticipating situations, they can prepare to act in a positive, productive manner instead of spending their energy dealing with the consequences of errors or inappropriate behavior. Do not allow students to resign themselves to the idea that they have no control or that their cases are hopeless.

- Students may need to learn how to use external controls, such as reminders from people and memory clues. A memory clue that helped one of my students who kept leaving her books behind was to practice stopping and looking around whenever she was about to exit a doorway. This became a habit and she left behind very few things thereafter.

- Students need to understand how racing thoughts reduce their ability to learn and do math. This self-awareness enables them to accept the techniques they need to use in order to learn. When students accept that they will make more mistakes than others, they won't be as resistant to developing the habit of checking assignments and test answers.

- Teach students to draw attention-getters (memory clues) to help them to remember all the steps in a sequence or math operation. Students write the attention-getter on the top of the test or assignment, or on a scrap paper, before beginning the task.

Adaptations and Accommodations

Sometimes students who have racing minds need more than remediation. Here's how you can adapt your instruction to help them do their best.

- Present material in small parts so students don't become overwhelmed or race to get everything done quickly.

- Use attention-getters (words, symbols, pictures) on test papers and assignments to remind students to check their work.

- Use key words as attention-getters. Print key words (such as "focus" or "zero in") on student papers, bookmarks, or classroom displays.

- Students with attention problems have individual needs. Give them frequent breaks, a quiet place to work, or background sounds like music, depending on their needs.

- Give students the extra time they need to complete tests or assignments so that they can carefully check their answers.

- Provide checklists and sequential steps so that students complete math tasks without drifting off or being distracted.

- If possible, supply students with talking calculators. Talking calculators provide an auditory check on the numbers and operations that students key in (see *Using Calculators* at the end of this chapter).

- Add checkpoint boxes to assignments and tests (as in *Figure 2.2*). Students draw a checkmark in the boxes when they have completed checking each section of their work.

Reading

Some students have learning problems that limit their acquisition of both language and math skills. Reading problems can exacerbate math problems. Students who cannot read the directions or comprehend the stories in word problems have difficulty completing math work independently. They also cannot learn effectively from textbooks and are often unable to review lessons on their own.

Remediations

In addition to increasing instruction in reading, you can provide assistance to students in math class using the following techniques.

▶ Have students collect and study math terms until they become part of their sight-reading vocabulary. Vocabulary can be collected from math textbooks and from word problems.

▶ Reading disabilities often make it difficult for students to improve their skills without direct instruction. Provide students with an audiotape of math terms that matches a written list so that they can listen and read the words until they are mastered.

▶ Use math textbooks and word problems as reading material in reading classes and tutoring sessions.

▶ Have students "collect" vocabulary words in a list in the back of their notebooks.

Adaptations and Accommodations

▶ Adapt math materials by reducing the amount of reading that is needed to complete the activities.

▶ Add illustrations to word problems to help students comprehend the text.

▶ Present instruction and exams orally so that students are being tested on their math skills, not their reading ability.

▶ Use audio materials to help students practice independently.

▶ Give students extra time to complete assignments and tests.

Right/Left Discrimination

Students who have right/left discrimination problems find it difficult to learn and remember items that are similar or opposite. For example, students find it difficult to remember whether *8 x 7 = 54 or 8 x 7 = 56* because *54* and *56* are similar. Inverting numbers in fractions is another example of a problem caused by right/left confusion. Right/left confusion is not a perception problem, but rather a problem of labeling and recording.

Right/left confusion causes what is commonly referred to as reversal; however, the term reversal often refers to mirror-image difficulties, such as reversing *b* and *d*. This use of the term misses most of the problems caused by right/left confusion. Instead of using the term *reversal*, use the term **confusable (either/or)**. This makes it easier to understand the thought process and the errors that result.

Spatial Relations

Jim was apprehensive about beginning high school because he heard that the high school grounds were difficult to navigate. Because of a right/left discrimination impairment, Jim had a tendency to get lost in malls and large parking lots, so he was sure that he was going to have difficulty finding his way around his new school.

Jim did in fact have difficulty navigating the high school building. The school, which was laid out in pods, was confusing until one became familiar with a few landmarks (e.g., the cafeteria, music room, and gym). Most ninth-graders learned their way in two or three days, but after two weeks Jim still arrived late for some classes.

One day Jim arrived late for math tutoring and expressed his frustration with the school grounds. I asked Jim to draw a map of the school. His map was very different than the actual layout of the school. I helped Jim redraw his map with the landmarks. Within a few days, he was getting to all his classes on time.

Students who have right/left discrimination problems experience confusion when processing or communicating concepts that include either/or relationships. The three areas in my classroom in which I have observed right/left discrimination problems are:

- Spatial relations (not knowing which way to turn)

- Language (confusing letters and words)

- Quantity (confusing numbers and concepts).

Impairments in the right/left discrimination thought process can cause reversals, thought process (memory) problems, and confusion.

Either/or confusion (or reversal) is caused by processing and communication problems—not perception problems. Students who read *b* instead of *d* do not see *b*. They see *d*, just like everyone else, but because of the right/left confusion, they do not know whether it is a *b* or a *d*. Another example of right/left confusion is when students write *E* instead of *3*. They do not see a *3*; they see exactly what they wrote, an *E*, but they do not remember if it is called *3* or *E*.

Right/left confusion is easier to understand if you consider young children who confuse their right and left sides. Many children put their shoes on the wrong feet, write numbers and letters backward, and confuse items that are similar. Each involves the same right/left confusion: *Either* this shoe goes on this foot *or* it goes on the other; you write this number *either* by going to the right or to the left. Children are not born with the ability to distinguish between right and left, to make right and left turns, or to distinguish between concepts that have either/or relationships. These are learned skills. However, some students take longer to move through developmental stages. Others have the confusion throughout their lives.

Right/left confusion is a thought process in which students continually focus on either/or possibilities rather than approaching problems and ideas from a new direction. Let's return to the *b/d* and *E/3* examples. Students who are not sure if a letter is *b* or *d* continue to try to decide whether the letter is *b* or *d* instead of accessing their motor memory of writing the letter. The students neither think of another word that begins with the same letter shape, nor use memory clues to remember which is which. The more the students try to distinguish between the letters, the more confused they become. The end result is either frustration or a guess. If students guess incorrectly, frequently they will not be aware of the error. If students guess correctly, it does not mean that any learning has taken place. The next time the same task is encountered, they find themselves in the same quandary.

Students usually master whether to move to the right or left when writing *3* by developing a motor memory. The memory is reinforced by teachers and parents who correct students every time they write *E* instead of *3*.

The either/or thought process is a geometric progression of thoughts. For example, when confronted with the multiplication problem *8 x 7*, students follow a line of reasoning like the one depicted in *Figure 2.3*:

   8 x 7 is either *54* or *56*.

   54 is either the product of *8 x 7* or the product of *9 x 6*.

   But 56 is either the product of *8 x 7* or the product of *9 x 6*.

At this point either students take a guess or continue to ponder the problem, going back and forth between *54* and *56* and *8 x 7* and *9 x 6*. They remain stuck, repeating the same thought process over and over.

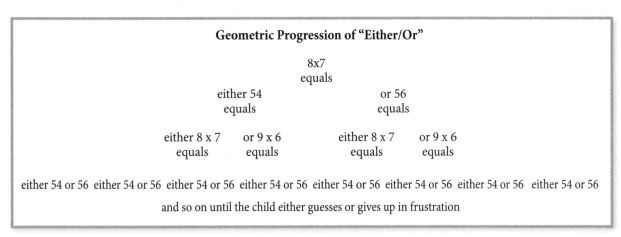

Figure 2.3: The geometric progression of an either/or thought process.

Only when students are sure that the either/or dilemma is solved does learning take place. Even then, if the correct answer is not reinforced immediately and frequently, the item learned will fade back into the confusion of either/or. In this way, right/left discrimination problems affect memory.

It is not uncommon for students to appear to learn something, even using it for a short period of time, and later appear as if they never learned it. For example, students who guess that a number is even, when it is odd, and are corrected by the teacher, may be able to remember for the rest of the class or school day that the number is odd. The next day, however, they will guess again because no learning took place. Until students are able to distinguish between the either/or aspects of the item, they cannot learn it. The correct information may reside in short-term memory, but it does not move to long-term memory.

Reversal is the most visible type of reading and writing problem, so it has become associated with dyslexia. However, reversal does not automatically indicate dyslexia or any kind of reading problem. Although many students with reading problems do manifest reversals, not all of them make reversals. Likewise, many students with right/left discrimination problems reverse a variety of things; however, they do not reverse letters or words and are excellent readers. Their reversals may be observed in confusion of spatial relationships, numbers, or quantitative concepts.

Many, if not all, students confuse right and left during their development. For most, it does not take long before they are able to remember their right and left sides or to remember which way to form letters and numbers. But this natural developmental process is delayed, or is nonexistent, for students who have problems with right/left discrimination.

Many students who exhibit problems with reversals seem to outgrow them. This is why it was believed for many years that students outgrow learning disabilities. When students' reversals fade, it is assumed that the problem has been corrected. But this is not always the case. The same thought process that causes reversals later makes it difficult for students to distinguish between terms, such as *subjective* and *objective*, that have either/or relationships. Other terms that have either/or relationships that are commonly confused (reversed) are:

- *Clockwise* and *counterclockwise*
- *Convex* and *concave*
- *Defense* and *offense*
- *Inductive reasoning* and *deductive reasoning*
- *Greater than* and *less than*
- *Numerators* and *denominators*
- *Odd* and *even*
- *Positive* and *negative*.

Right/left discrimination problems, which are most often observed as reversals in reading and writing, include the less obvious confusion of vocabulary and concepts. Students do not outgrow the either/or thought process. It matures with them.

Confusion between o*dd* and *even* is a good example of a right/left discrimination problem that affects skills at higher levels. Often teachers are not concerned when students cannot remember odd and even numbers in the early grades. However, without the concepts of odd and even, many students do not see patterns in numbers. Additionally, because students do not know that the addition and subtraction of like numbers (odd or even) result in an even number, they aren't able to check their work using this pattern. Students then rely on guessing to determine answers. And when they guess, students can only check their answers by guessing again. (Students earnestly believe they are checking their work by guessing again!)

Remediations

▶ First and foremost, students with right/left discrimination problems must understand their own thought process. Students who make reversals or have difficulty learning items that are similar or opposite usually will say, "It's because I am stupid." This belief lowers students' self-esteem and leads to patterns of avoidance ("Why should I try if I am so stupid?"). When students understand that right/left confusion is part of a thought process that is both positive and negative, they can modify their negative self-images to positive ones. Understanding their thought process allows students to more easily see both sides of an issue, thereby enhancing creativity and enabling students to be more tolerant of others with differences.

Students who previously felt stupid or helpless begin to feel adequate and in control.

▶ The second step in helping students with right/left discrimination problems is to teach them techniques that remove the either/or dilemma and help them remember differences between items that are similar.

▶ One technique that removes the either/or dilemma is **weighted learning**. This technique for learning and remembering involves learning one side of an either/or rather than both sides. With odd and even numbers, the student only learns the even numbers of *2, 4, 6, 8,* and *0*. When a number is not one of these, then the number is odd.

▶ The use of mnemonics is another technique for dealing with right/left discrimination problems. There are commonly known mnemonics (**Every good boy does fine** for the lines of a musical staff or **Please excuse my dear Aunt Sally** for the order of operations), and there are those that are custom-made to help students learn and remember things. Mnemonics that are used in conjunction with weighted learning are most effective; for example, the *d* in denominator is associated with the word ***down***. With weighted learning, you do not create mnemonic clues for both parts of an "either/or" because this leads to the confusion of the clues. For example, one teacher tried to help a student remember odd and even by showing the even numbers as happy faces and the odd numbers as ugly faces. The student still could not remember odd and even because he could not remember if odd numbers or even numbers were ugly faces. The teacher could not understand why her technique did not work. To her it was obvious that odd was associated with ugly, but it was not obvious to the student.

▶ Another technique for helping students break either/or confusion is prioritizing. Prioritizing is particularly effective for decision-making and problem-solving. Many students who have right/left discrimination problems find it difficult to make up their minds. A trip to the store can be an agonizing experience, not only for the students with the problem, but also for those who accompany them. Take, for example, Mary. She could not make up her mind about which kind of bread to buy. She spent much time trying to decide if she should buy white or wheat bread, this brand or that, the cheap or expensive brand, the regular size or the king size. By learning to prioritize ahead of time, Mary learned to choose a loaf of bread quickly and easily. She decided that cost was her first concern, then wheat was her preference, and finally that she would always buy the larger loaf when it was available.

▶ Students may have difficulty deciding what to do first when trying to solve a problem. Without a predetermined set of steps, they attempt to solve problems in different ways, sometimes choosing the correct way and other times not.

▶ Some students are able to use conceptualization and association as a way to reduce right/left confusion and improve memory. Using the example of odd and even numbers again, we can see that if a student is able to understand that even numbers are pairs, then numbers which are not part of a pair are odd.

▶ Learning items in a series instead of in pairs is another technique. For example, when working with students who are confused by the operations involved in solving fractions, teach the operations of addition, subtraction, multiplication and division as a set rather than individually.

▶ Students who possess the right/left discrimination thought process frequently exhibit the Continuum of the Absolute. This phenomenon is observed in students who have difficulty with absolute terms like *never, always, total, sum,* etc. Instead of understanding these terms as absolutes, students understand them as continuums from some to all. The concept of *never* is understood as a continuum from *never-now* to *never-never*.

▶ Repetition sometimes reduces the number of reversals and confusions. However, stress, fatigue, time pressure, performance pressure, and anxiety exacerbate right/left confusion, reducing any gain obtained by repetition.

▶ Students who have right/left discrimination problems often make reversals (transpositions) such as writing *61* for *16* or *27* for *72*. One way to reduce reversals is to eliminate crossing from left to right when copying numbers. Students can place the book or material that they are copying above their notebooks rather than to the side (as in *Figure 2.4*).

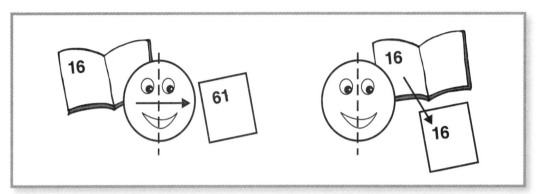

Figure 2.4: Copying work from above rather than the side reduces reversal.

Adaptations and Accommodations

Students who struggle with right/left discrimination are often misunderstood. Parents and teachers sometimes interpret their confusion as lack of focus, dislike for a subject, insufficient study, or some other attitudinal problem.

▶ Right/left discrimination problems make it difficult to distinguish between items that are similar or opposite, so be sure to avoid asking true-or-false questions.

▶ Also avoid multiple-choice questions because students eventually must choose between two answers.

▶ Evaluate achievement by having students demonstrate skills rather than having them answer true-or-false or multiple-choice questions.

Accommodate students by providing:

▶ Alternative assignments and test formats.

▶ Calculators to complete calculations and/or check answers (also see *Using Calculators* at the end of this chapter).

▶ Extra time to complete assignments and examinations.

Sequencing

Sequencing difficulty (e.g., in multiple-step multiplication or division problems) is not a frequent learning problem, but it can cause many problems. Sequencing errors include skipping steps, adding steps, and mixing up steps. These errors are compounded by the confusion caused by the sequencing difficulty: Students are unable to find or correct their errors.

Remediations

Students who have problems with sequencing need to learn to make and use memory tools. Try the following techniques.

▶ Teach students to make checklists when faced with any sequence that they find difficult to understand or remember. Checklists provide reference information and ensure that each step of a sequence is completed in the correct order. *Figure 2.5* shows an example of a checklist students can use for long division.

Figure 2.5: An example of a sequence checklist.

▶ **Use acronyms.** Help students to remember complex sequences and keep them separate from other sequences by creating a word or a pseudo-word from the first letter of each step.

▶ **Try visualizations.** An example of a visualization is given in Chapter 9, *Visual Clue: Swimming Pool*. This clue helps students remember the sequence of operations to change fractions to decimals.

▶ **Give mnemonic clues.** Students better remember concepts, operations, and sequences (especially those that are not used frequently) when they have mnemonic clues. Some mnemonic clues are widely known and used, but you can also custom-make clues for individual students. Better yet, teach students to create their own mnemonic clues so that they become more independent learners.

▶ Set up physical locations for each step in a process. Students go to each location to complete the steps. For example, tape five lines on the floor for the five steps of solving word problems (see *Figure 4.32*) and let the students walk to each line when solving a word problem.

Adaptations and Accommodations

Students usually do not know how to approach problems in sequential ways, so format math assignments and tests to help them be sequential. Try the following ideas.

▶ Break down assignments into step-by-step operations to guide students who are having problems sequencing.

▶ Post checklists, acronyms, visualizations, and mnemonic clues in plain sight in the classroom or tape them to students' desks. Or, if you want to be less obvious, write them on students' notebooks or on bookmarks so that they have ready access to the steps they need to complete math operations.

▶ Allow students more time to complete assignments and tests.

Visual Perception and Processing

One common visual perception problem is an impaired ability to distinguish between foreground and background. Students with this kind of impairment may have difficulty interpreting graphs and laying out information in written form. Foreground/background impairments may even affect students' perceptions of where the edge of their papers are and can cause students to write on a slant or irregularly across the page. Students who have visual perception and processing problems often have difficulty properly spacing letters and numbers when writing. They may also have difficulty lining up numbers in columns when completing math operations. Sometimes students can also be distracted by color, paying attention to some items and ignoring others.

Remediations

▸ Always refer students who are having difficulty seeing to a professional for a visual screening. They may need corrective lenses. Even with glasses or contacts, however, students may experience difficulty with some visual tasks.

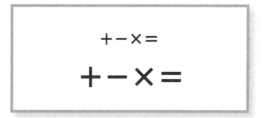

Figure 2.6: Making mathematical symbols bold helps students pay closer attention.

▸ One visual problem is inattention to symbols. To remedy this, teach students to bold the symbols when doing math operations, as in *Figure 2.6*.

▸ Teach students to use specific colors for activities. For example, in solving a long division problem, they may use blue when completing a multiplication computation and red when subtracting. Although using colors adds time to the task, many students find it to be an effective way to understand and keep track of the operations. The resulting pattern also increases the ease of checking their completed work.

▸ Standardized-test answer sheets, or bubble sheets, present a special problem for students who have difficulty with visual tracking. Ensure that students mark their answers in the correct spaces by having them practice filling in the bubbles using rulers, bookmarks, or other straight edges. This helps them track across the page.

▸ Another way to provide practice with standardized-tests is to increase the size of the test pages and answer sheets on a photocopier (as in *Figure 2.7*). Have students practice filling in the enlarged answer sheets until they can fill them out accurately. Then, gradually decrease the size until it is normal.

Practice: Add or subtract.

1. $ 8.54	2. $ 5.42	3. $ 0.98
+ 0.23	+ 4.68	+ 0.49

4. $ 5.99	5. $ 79.18	6. $ 46.49
+ 0.17	+ 32.82	+ 24.77

1. $ 8.54	2. $ 5.42	3. $ 0.98
+ 0.23	+ 4.68	+ 0.49

4. $ 5.99	5. $ 79.18	6. $ 46.49
+ 0.17	+ 32.82	+ 24.77

Figure 2.7: Enlarging test pages on a photocopier can help students read and complete the problems correctly.

Adaptations and Accommodations

▶ The primary adaptation for general vision problems is to use materials in large-print formats. This adaptation is easy to provide because most photocopiers have an enlargement function. When you assign text pages or worksheets, enlarge them first for students.

▶ Position materials using paper mounts and bookstands so that students can read them more easily.

▶ Scan your math materials into a computer, increasing the size of the font. Students can complete the problems on-screen, or you can print a hard copy with the larger font for students to complete.

▶ Use graph paper to assist students with visual perception and processing problems.

▶ Adapt math exercises and tests by providing students with bold symbols to help them focus their attention on these symbols.

▶ When you are preparing materials, use a computer to color code them.

▶ Adapt answer sheets that require students to fill in small circles or rectangles by making them larger. Reduce them later for computerized scoring.

▶ Students who have visual perception and processing problems may need:

- Someone to mark their answer sheets.
- Oral formats for assignments and examinations.
- Extra time to complete assignments and examinations.

Using Calculators

There is much discussion among educators about the use of calculators as a substitute for learning basic math skills. Some students naturally learn and understand basic math concepts and number facts whether they use calculators or not. Others have difficulty learning concepts. These students have even more difficulty later on if they do not grasp basic number facts and operations of arithmetic.

A middle-of-the-road instructional approach is probably the most useful for students with weak math skills and/or learning problems. When working with these students, teach them:

- Basic number facts and how to use them to solve simple calculations.

- How to use a calculator to solve more complex calculations.

Because students with learning problems make more mistakes than their peers without problems, it is critical that they learn to check their answers. When students are taught to use calculators for checking even simple calculations, they can find and correct errors on their own. Over time, they learn the number facts and math operations.

Special Displays and Keys

Some students need strong visual cues. They need large displays to see the numbers they enter into their calculators. Others have motor challenges that make small calculators a source of frustration. Be sure that the calculators these students use have large number-keys and sizable character displays as in *Figure 2.8*. In addition, multiline displays and/or paper printouts can further reduce errors.

Also consider the number of functions that a calculator performs. As a general rule, students should use the simplest calculator available for the level of math they are learning. This makes the calculator easier to operate and reduces the opportunities for accidentally touching incorrect keys.

When teaching students to use calculators, be sure to teach them to check the answer the calculator gives them by comparing it to their own estimate. Some students have difficulty using calculators because they do not have adequate estimating skills. They trust the calculator without question, and so do not catch errors even when the calculator's answer is way off.

Figure 2.8: Students with visual and/or motor difficulties do best when using calculators with large displays and keys, like this one.

Talking Calculators

Talking calculators, like the one in *Figure 2.9*, pronounce each number and operation as it is entered and then say the answer. They are excellent assistive devices for students who have racing minds or need auditory reinforcement. The auditory "display" helps students to check that they have keyed in the correct numbers and functions. For example, a student may mean to enter the number *53* but trigger to the next number, *54*. With an ordinary calculator this error is easily overlooked, but with a talking calculator, the number is announced: "54." The student is alerted to the error and can try again. The talking function also helps students when they accidentally press the wrong function key. If they press the division key instead of the multiplication key, the calculator says "divided by." Students can catch their mistakes before they finish a math problem.

Figure 2.9: Many students benefit from the auditory reinforcement that talking calculators provide.

Helping Students Learn Number Facts

This chapter will help you ameliorate some of the specific difficulties students have when learning number facts (the single-digit combinations used in the operations of addition, subtraction, multiplication, and division; e.g., 1 + 1 = 2, 3 – 2 = 1, 4 x 4 = 16, $9\overline{)81}$. This chapter focuses on memory and patterns rather than on conventional methods, such as. concept development, problem-solving, and using manipulatives. Working with memory and patterns is not a substitute for methodology, but it can be a highly effective supplement to the instructional strategies you already use. When students are evidencing computation errors or weak quantitative concepts, or are performing poorly on assignments and tests, it can be helpful to understand the differences in how students access their math knowledge.

The Hierarchy of Number-Fact Skills

There are distinct differences in how students remember the basic number facts of addition, subtraction, multiplication, and division. Students who have poor math skills often use different techniques to recall number facts than their math-proficient peers do. *Figure 3.1*, developed from my clinical observations, ranks the eight skills (or thought processes) students use to access number facts to solve math problems.

Eight Ways to Access Number Facts

1. Automatically recalling number facts

2. Recalling number facts (delayed)

3. Converting to reverse operations

4. Using number relationships

5. Referring to mnemonic clues

6. Counting or sequencing correctly

7. Guessing number facts

8. Counting or sequencing (with error)

Source: Cooper, Richard. Teaching Math Instructional Guide. Bryn Mawr, PA: Learning disAbilities Resources, 1996.

Figure 3.1: The hierarchy of number-fact skills students use to solve math problems.

Automatically recalling number facts. When students automatically recall number facts (without hesitation), they have mastered them. When asked to solve 5 + 5 =, most high school students automatically respond "10." The response is as automatic as flinching when surprised. Some students, especially those who have natural ability in math, automatically recall all the number facts. Most students automatically recall some number facts. Students with significant math weaknesses, however, may only be able to recall a few number facts automatically.

Solving math problems with many digits requires multiple computations. Each computation requires a number fact, and each number fact takes time to recall. For students who automatically recall number facts, computations take a minimum amount of time.

Recalling number facts (delayed). Sometimes students know the number facts, but they must think for a moment before they are able to recall them. They do not need mnemonic devices or other cues to remember the facts, just a moment or two to recall them. This delayed recall may be due to the way students process the information. When students are asked to add, subtract, multiply, or divide two numbers, they may visualize the numbers on a page as a way to remember the answer. Or students may say the numbers to themselves as a way of remembering the answer. Both of these processes create a delay in automatic recall. These students take more time to complete the computation than their peers who automatically recall number facts.

Converting to reverse operations. Sometimes students access number facts by recalling an opposite function (e.g., using multiplication to solve a division problem). Using reverse operations differs from automatic recall in that students recall the opposite fact first, then reverse it to arrive at the answer. For example, when a student encounters *15 – 8 =*, he thinks *8 + 7 = 15*, and then responds that the answer is *7*. Likewise, to solve *42 ÷ 6 =*, a student reverses to *7 x 6 = 42*, then responds *6*.

Using number relationships. The fourth level of knowledge in the number fact hierarchy is that of number relationships. At this level, students use the number facts they know in order to determine the number facts in question. For example, to solve *8 + 6 =*, students automatically recall *8 + 8 = 16*. Then they subtract *2* to arrive at *14*. To solve *9 + 7 =*, students change the *9* to *10*, and add the *7*, to get *17*. Then they subtract *1* to arrive at *16*. Using number relationships to solve problems involves more than one computation, so it takes longer to use than automatic recall, delayed recall, or reverse operations.

Referring to mnemonic clues. Mnemonic clues are visual, auditory, and/or tactile clues that help students remember number facts. They include music, rhymes, visualizations, language clues, and movements—anything that helps students remember. One student said that she remembered the number fact *7 + 7 = 14* by relating it to two touchdowns in football with the total score of *14*.

Although processing number facts using mnemonic clues is quick, few students use them. Unfortunately, mnemonic clues are often considered tricks or crutches, implying that they are an undesirable way to learn the facts. Mnemonic clues can make the difference between quick, correct recall, and slow (and sometimes incorrect) calculations of number facts.

Counting correctly. Many students count to calculate number facts when they do not know them. They use their fingers, count silently to themselves, or make marks on paper and then count the marks. They may be able to automatically recall *5 + 5 = 10* but count on their fingers to solve *5 + 6*. Counting takes much longer than automatically recalling facts, significantly slowing down the computations of multiple-digit operations. The longer time it requires often leads to frustration and a sense that math is difficult, tedious, and time consuming.

Guessing number facts. Some students guess what the number facts are. They often make errors and frequently believe that their guesses are correct even when they are not. These students have no other way of obtaining answers. Eventually they stop caring or they give up.

Guessing tends to increase when students are under pressure to perform or when they are in a hurry. Pressure is often associated with tests and completing tasks while being observed. Guessing precludes checking one's answers. How do you check a guess? Guess again?

Counting (with error). Some students make errors when counting to calculate the number facts. Students who have difficulty sequencing may skip numbers as they count. Students with right/left discrimination problems may not remember whether to begin counting on or after the number. For example, 8 + 5 = 13, but if students start counting on 8 instead of 9, the answer they arrive at is 12. Besides taking longer than the other number-fact skills, errors in counting leave students feeling like they just can't learn math.

Helping Students Move Up the Hierarchy

There is a natural progression from the bottom to the top of the hierarchy of number-fact skills. Usually students who automatically recall number facts not only possess a natural ability in math, but also have an understanding of quantitative concepts, ample success with math, and spend sufficient time practicing. Students who have not achieved automaticity with all the number facts usually can recall some facts automatically (such as 2 + 2 = 4 and 5 + 5 = 10), but they often use lower-level skills to calculate the facts they use infrequently.

Some students never reach the first level of the hierarchy, automatic recall of all the number facts. This happens for many reasons. One reason is that anxiety (either performance anxiety or worry about everyday problems) results in a delay in recall. Another reason is that students who avoid math do not use the number facts enough to remember them all. Although these students may never achieve automatic recall, if they are not counting or guessing, but using other techniques for remembering number facts, they are completing computations quicker and more accurately than before.

When they are not addressed, learning differences can also result in not attaining automatic recall. Students who have right/left discrimination problems have difficulty remembering number facts. When counting, they cannot remember if they start on the number or on the next number. Students with racing minds often rush through math and make many guesses. Use the techniques provided in Chapter 2 to help students with these and other learning challenges master number facts.

The goal for all students who do not know the number facts by automatic recall is to move up the hierarchy. With practice and study, some students who have learning differences can reach the automatic recall level for all the addition, subtraction, multiplication, and division facts.

Many students may not achieve automatic recall for all the number facts, but if they are able to move beyond the bottom three levels of the hierarchy (counting, guessing, and counting with errors), they will be more successful in math. By using the top five levels of the hierarchy, students increase the speed and accuracy of their computations. As a result, their self-image in relation to math improves.

Teaching Basic Math Concepts

This chapter focuses on the basic math concepts I have found to be particularly challenging for students who have problems learning math. The instructional techniques are meant to supplement regular instruction, not supplant it. The math concepts are arranged alphabetically for ease of reference.

Counting

Although we expect students who are beyond the first few grades to be able to count with little or no difficulty, many students have deficits in sequencing or have learning differences that result in weak counting skills. Poor counting skills limit students' math development. Students with weak counting skills:

- Make errors of omission (skipping numbers), and/or

- Have problems with transitions from one pattern to another.

Examples of problems with transitions in counting are "forty-eight, forty-nine, forty-ten" and "998; 999; 1,000; 2,000; 3,000." Triggering, the phenomenon of jumping to the next logical thought, can occur during counting. Students think one number but say another. For example, a student might think *18* but say *80*. He then counts *16, 17, 80, 81, 82*. Students who have problems counting find themselves making inexplicable errors. They are left feeling, at best, inadequate or, at worst, stupid.

On a Personal Note:

Assessing Counting Skills

As a learning specialist, I assess students' information processing abilities. This specialized assessment often uncovers many gaps in basic skills. In particular, it uncovers gaps in counting. Gaps in counting are often an indication of significant problems with other math skills. Most students can count easily and quickly by fives up to 100. But when asked to count by fives beyond 100, many students look at me questioningly and ask how. I get them started, "105, 110, 115," and they count "116, 117" or "120, 200, 300." Most of these students have never counted by fives beyond 100.

Depending on student age and ability level, I ask students to count from 1 to 20 and backward from 10 or from 20. I have them count by twos, fives, tens, twenties, and twenty-fives. I ask older students to count larger numbers (such as by twos starting at 524 or by fives starting at 4,215). I give counting exercises to students who have difficulty counting to remediate their skills.

Why Is Counting Important?

Counting begins at an early age: two or three. At first, children are only imitating but, through many thousands of repetitions, they begin to understand the sequence of numbers and that the next number is larger than the one before it. Most children quickly learn that they can count the things that are the subjects of their attention (e.g., "There are four puppies."). A natural progression is for children to learn that they can count more quickly by twos or other intervals. By the time they are in school, children usually can count by twos, fives, and tens. They have learned the rhythm in those sequences. However, if students make mistakes counting, it can be difficult for them to take the next step: learning number facts. Counting exercises help students count without error so that they succeed at learning number facts later.

Counting Exercises

Counting exercises can be simple or complex. Students need to start practicing at the level at which they are having difficulty. Young students often have problems with the numbers between *10* and *20*. Older students have difficulty making transitions from one set of numbers to another, such as from *38, 39* to *40, 41* or from *99* to *100*. Students count *37, 38, 39* and stop because they cannot remember the next number. Or they count *87, 98, 99, 109, 110, 111*.

At a higher level, students need practice counting large numbers, such as beginning at *548* or *2,875*. Have students practice counting *548, 549, 550, 551*, continuing for a minute or so. Then have them begin another sequence (e.g., *2,875; 2,876; 2,877; 2,878*; etc.). These exercises help students to:

- Sequence numbers.

- Hear (recognize) the patterns in numbers.

- Improve their memory for holding multidigit numbers.

Counting exercises are best when completed both orally and in writing. Oral exercises help students to develop the language and rhythm of numbers, and written exercises help students to identify the patterns in numbers. Use the reproducibles on the *Alternative Math Techniques* CD to provide counting practice.

Counting by Intervals

Students are often able to count by twos, fives, and tens without much difficulty. Interval counting like this is the precursor of multiplication. Sometimes students have difficulty counting by these intervals, however, when asked to count beyond common sets of numbers (e.g., beyond *100*). If students can count beyond *100*, they count slowly, and/or begin to make errors of omission.

The exercises in *Figure 4.1*, arranged in order from most easy to most difficult, provide practice in counting by intervals. Counting by twos from *428*, an even number, is easier than counting from *1* because *1* is an odd number. Once students master counting by twos, they begin counting by fives, beginning with easier exercises and moving to more difficult ones. Counting exercises, like the ones in *Figure 4.1* and in the reproducibles, assist students with mental math and sequencing skills, and improve self-confidence.

Interval Counting Practice	
Exercise	**Directions**
1.	Beginning at 50, count by twos.
2.	Beginning at 428, count by twos.
3.	Beginning at 1, count by twos.
4.	Beginning at 265, count by fives.
5.	Beginning at 3,985; count by fives.
6.	Beginning at 10,125; count by fives.
7.	Beginning at 2, count by fives.

Figure 4.1: Practice counting by intervals teaches sequencing and sharpens mental math skills.

Counting by fives starting at *1, 2, 3,* or *4* gives students a sense of how numbers work. Understanding patterns helps students with arithmetic operations. Practicing counting by intervals also improves mental math skills. For example, when students encounter *67 + 5*, they can easily add them because the pattern of counting by fives (*67, 72, 77, 82*) is already in their memory.

Give students practice counting by tens, twenties, twenty-fives, fifties, and hundreds starting at various numbers. Students need to learn to count by twenty-fives in order to be able to count money. For more practice ideas for counting by intervals, see Chapter 7, *Counting Exercises*.

Counting Fractions

As stated in Chapter 2, *Right/Left Discrimination*, students who have difficulty with inversion often have problems with fractions. Fraction counting exercises familiarize students with the language of fractions and the rhythm of their patterns. Practicing the rhythm of *whole* and *part* provides a foundation for the learning of fractions. In *Figure 4.2* students repeat the fractions to learn the pattern.

The Language of Fractions	
whole and part	_____ *and* _____
one and a half	*one and three-fourths*
two and a third	*three and one-fifth*
five and three-eighths	*four and three-sixteenths*

Figure 4.2: Students repeat the fractions orally, understanding the pattern of whole and part.

When you introduce fraction-counting exercises, you may need to provide guides, like those listed in *Figure 4.3* and provided in the reproducibles as Math Concepts: Counting Fractions: Oral: Worksheet A. Students read the fraction guides until they are learned. The guides in *Figure 4.3* are in order from most easy to most difficult. In time, most students will be able to count without looking at their guides.

Guides for Counting Fractions		
Exercise	**Interval**	**Guide**
A.	Starting at 1/2, count by halves.	1/2, 1, 1 and 1/2, 2, 2 and 1/2, 3, 3 and 1/2, 4, 4 and 1/2 . . .
B.	Starting at 1/4, count by quarters.	1/4, 1/2, 3/4, 1, 1 and 1/4, 1 and 1/2, 1 and 3/4, 2, 2 and 1/4, 2 and 1/2, 2 and 3/4, 3 . . .
C.	Starting at 1/8, count by eighths.	1/8, 1/4, 3/8, 1/2, 5/8, 3/4, 7/8, 1, 1 and 1/8, 1 and 1/4, 1 and 3/8, 1 and 1/2, 1 and 5/8, 1 and 3/4, 1 and 7/8, 2 . . .
D.	Starting at 1/3, count by thirds.	1/3, 2/3, 1, 1 and 1/3, 1 and 2/3, 2, 2 and 1/3, 2 and 2/3, 3, 3 and 1/3, 3 and 2/3, 4 . . .
E.	Starting at 1/16, count by sixteenths.	1/16, 1/8, 3/16, 1/4, 5/16, 3/8, 7/16, 1/2, 9/16, 5/8, 11/16, 3/4, 13/16, 7/8, 15/16, 1 . . .
F.	Starting at 0.5, count by halves.	.5, 1, 1.5, 2, 2.5, 3, 3.5, 4, 4.5, 5, 5.5, 6 . . .
G.	Starting at 0.1, count by tenths.	.1, .2, .3, .4, .5, .6, .7, .8, .9, 1, 1.1, 1.2, 1.3, 1.4, 1.5, 1.6, 1.7, 1.8, 1.9, 2, 2.1, 2.2, 2.3 . . .

Figure 4.3: When introducing students to fraction counting exercises, give them guides like these.

Estimating

Students who do not understand the concept of estimating often believe that estimating means guessing. They believe that answers to math problems are either right or wrong, so they are confused by the concept of estimating. It takes a lot of practice for them to become good estimators.

You can help students improve their estimation skills by helping them to use common objects to estimate measurements. Show them how to measure close to an inch with the knuckles of their fingers and one foot with part of their arms. Teach students the approximate height of tables, chairs, doors, and other objects in the classroom and at home, using the *Estimating* reproducibles on the *Alternative Math Techniques* CD. Ask them if they know the size of common ceiling and floor tiles, concrete blocks, and wall panels. As students become familiar with the measurements of the things around them, they gain points of reference for estimating.

Math Language

Students with poor math skills often have underdeveloped and ambiguous vocabularies. Be aware that students may not understand the words you are using to describe math concepts. Concrete thinkers, who often have a limited understanding of abstract terms, often do not understand math terms. They may also have difficulty using common words in new contexts. For example, they may understand the word *area* to mean a general space, as in *picnic area*, but not be able to comprehend the mathematical meaning of *area* as a space having length and width.

Some students develop language skills at a slower rate than others or do not clearly hear the sounds in words. They lag behind in vocabulary development because it takes them longer to learn new words—especially abstract concepts that they cannot use their senses to understand. They have no problem understanding the word *table* because they can see and touch it, but they have difficulty with the word *complementary* as it relates to angles.

Figure 4.4 shows the vocabulary growth of two students. The upper line indicates the vocabulary of Student A, who does not have learning difficulties. The lower line shows the vocabulary of Student B, who has auditory perception problems. As the gap between the two lines widens, Student B has increasing difficulty understanding oral and written information.

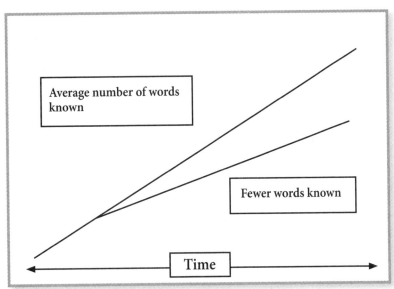

Figure 4.4: As the vocabulary gap widens, Student B falls further behind.

Words that represent concepts that change are difficult for these students to learn. The word *whole* is one such word. Concretely, the *whole* pizza is easy to understand, but seeing and understanding 25 beans as a *whole* is problematic. Students who understand *double* to mean *more*, and *half* to mean *less*, often remain confused about these concepts for years. Likewise, students who understand *reduce* to mean *make smaller* may think that *4/8* is larger than *1/2* because they *reduce* it to *1/2*.

The first thing to do is to note exactly what students understand about specific words and concepts. Question them in private to reduce any sense of embarrassment. If a student's response is humorous, or even outrageous, do not show shock or dismay about the misunderstanding. Maintain your composure throughout the questioning so that students aren't embarrassed.

Once you know which terms students need help with, you can help sharpen their vocabulary and focus their attention on the words using the *Math Language* reproducibles on the CD. You don't need to single out students. All students benefit from vocabulary posters that display new terms and give clues for remembering meanings. Students can increase their vocabulary through the regular and systematic study of words. Set up a system for students to "collect" words, then create assignments that use those words. Students can collect key words, new words, or words that are confusing on a special vocabulary bookmark. Bookmarks work well because they are readily available for students to reference and add to.

On a Personal Note:

Back-Page Vocabulary

Students who have underdeveloped vocabularies and poor organizational skills benefit from this simple technique. Have them take notes and complete assignments only on the front sides of their notebook pages. Have them reserve the back of the pages for vocabulary. When students encounter a new word, or you encounter one that they do not fully understand, have them write the word on the back of the pages, beginning from the back of the notebook. Have students list only one or two words per page so that there is room to write definitions, sentences using the word, and examples and illustrations that will help the students understand the words.

Measuring

Students who exhibit significant difficulty with measuring usually continue to exhibit this difficulty throughout their lives. They never acquire the skill. Students have difficulty measuring for three reasons:

- They do not fully understand and read scales.

- They do not understand units of measurement.

- They are confused about fractions.

Difficulty with measuring may be the result of only one of these three, or it may be due to two or all three of them.

Understanding and Reading Scales

Figure 4.5a shows a typical ruler used in classrooms. Notice that the numbers on the ruler are to the left of the inch marks. Students who are not familiar with the scale of this ruler may assume that the location of the inch is directly *above* the number (not to the side). This assumption results in errors when complete measuring tasks but, more significantly, it causes confusion about fractions of the unit. If students believe that the one-inch mark is directly above the *1*, then they assume the half-inch mark is before the actual half-inch mark (as in *Figure 4.5b*). They believe correctly that the half-inch mark is halfway between the whole numbers, but because they began measuring from the wrong point, everything is off.

Figure 4.5a: A typical ruler used by students learning to measure.

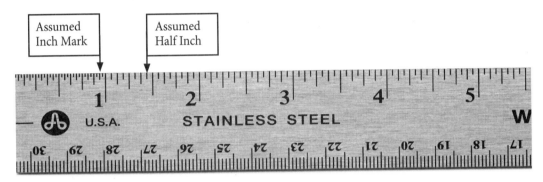

Figure 4.5b: The same ruler, as used by a student who assumes the 1-inch mark is above the 1.

The printer's ruler in *Figure 4.6* shows numbers next to the inch marks, but the numbers for the picas are on the lines. This shows that, although numbers are typically next to the unit marks when working in inches, there is no inherent reason for this practice.

Figure 4.6: A typical printer's ruler measure.

If available, use rulers and other measuring instruments that have numbers under the inch marks instead of next to them, as in *Figure 4.7*. If these are not available, you can modify rulers by extending the inch marks all the way across the ruler to emphasize where they are located. Then label the half-inch marks as illustrated in *Figure 4.8*.

Figure 4.7: Rulers that are designed for instruction reduce measuring errors.

Figure 4.8: Modify existing rulers to reduce measuring errors by extending the inch marks and writing 1/2 at the half-inch marks.

You can further demystify measuring by first teaching students to measure with approximate measures, then you can gradually increase the precision of their measurements. Start students off by having them measure items in their environment and rounding to the nearest inch. When students have mastered measuring to the nearest inch, introduce the concept of the half-inch. Use the *Measuring* reproducibles on the *Alternative Math Techniques* CD to provide practice.

Understanding Units of Measure

Students who are concrete thinkers or who have limited understanding of quantitative concepts are likely to have difficulty with units of measure. They may be able to name units (such as inch, foot, and yard) but may not understand that each unit is a whole. The idea that an inch is a unit that can be divided into parts, a foot is a unit that can be divided into parts, and that other units can also be divided into parts is a concept that eludes many students of all ages.

Students who think concretely have difficulty with the concept of a *unit*. They may grasp that there are 12 parts in a foot but not understand that in another unit, a pound, there are 16 parts.

Likewise, students who do not understand quantitative concepts will not understand that a quart is one-fourth of a gallon. They need these concepts and terms taught and reinforced repeatedly until they fully understand them and they become part of their vocabulary. Use the *Units of Measure* reproducibles on the CD to provide practice.

One way to ingrain measurement terms and concepts in students is to make the terms visible and commonplace. You can do this by displaying mobiles of units of measure in proportionate ways. For example, create a yardstick mobile with three one-foot rulers hanging from it, and 12 inches hanging from each ruler. You can also construct mobiles using gallon containers, half-gallons, quarts, pints, and cups. When terms and concepts of units become commonplace in your classroom, students have a chance to grasp them and use them in daily activities.

Cutting Through the Confusion of Fractions

Measuring fractions of units is particularly difficult for students who do not understand the sequence of fractions. Some students read fractions on a ruler in the following manner:

1/4 1/2 1/4 **1** 1/4 1/2 1/4 **2** 1/4 1/2 1/4 **3** 1/4 1/2 1/4 **4** 1/4 1/2 1/4 **5** 1/4 1/2 1/4 **6** 1/4 1/2 1/4 **7** 1/4 1/2 1/4 **8**

Students who read rulers in this way do not understand quarters and are confused by eighths.

Another problem students have with fractions of units is that they do not understand wholes and parts. Students may identify *3/4* of an inch as *3 1/4* inches.

You can assist students who have difficulty with the sequence of fractions by having them practice the fraction-counting exercise in the *Counting* section of this chapter. When students can easily count in quarters (see *Figure 4.3, Exercise B*), they can more easily learn to measure to the nearest quarter-inch. Then have students practice counting by eighths (*Figure 4.3, Exercise C*) and, if necessary, by sixteenths (*Figure 4.3, Exercise E*). When students are familiar with the pattern and rhythm of counting these fractions, they will be able to learn to measure with a ruler and other measuring instruments.

Ask students (who have already learned to round to the nearest inch) to measure and record their results to the nearest half-inch. Then introduce the quarter-inch. This usually requires more instruction and practice. When students have mastered measuring to the nearest quarter-inch, introduce the eighth-inch and, if necessary, the sixteenth-inch and smaller. As the fractions get smaller, students need more instruction and practice to master the measurement.

Money

There are few skills in our society as necessary as counting money, yet many students are not proficient in the basic skills needed to engage in money exchange. Students who have difficulty learning to count money usually have difficulty with:

- Coin values (inversion)
- Interval counting (especially by twenty-fives)
- Making change.

Students may have problems in all three of these areas or in only one. When problems arise, the underlying basic skills must be addressed in order to bring students up to speed.

Coin Values (Inversion)

Learning the value of the nickel and the dime is problematic for students who have right/left discrimination problems because of the inversion: The nickel is larger in size than the dime, yet has a lower value. Use **weighted learning** to teach the value of *either* the nickel or the dime (not both). Then have students practice to mastery before introducing the other coin. If students become confused, remind them to recall the first one learned. For more about weighted learning, see Chapter 2, *Right/Left Discrimination, Remediations.*

Counting by Intervals

Less obvious than inversion, and longer-lasting (even into adolescence and adulthood), are problems with counting by intervals. Students who cannot count by twenty-fives (quarters) count money beginning with the coins that they can count (e.g., nickels and dimes). Then they have to mentally add in the quarters—a much more difficult task.

When given the change in *Figure 4.9*, most people start counting with the quarter, add the nickel, the dime, and then the penny. They count: *$0.25, $0.30, $0.40, and $0.41.* But students who do not know how to count by twenty-fives start counting the coins they know how to count: nickels, dimes, and pennies. The students then count: *$0.10, $0.15, $0.16,* and now have to add *$0.25* in order to get to *$0.41.* If they do not have paper and pencil handy, they soon learn that they cannot count money. The result is that, when they pay sales clerks with bills, they have to trust the clerks to give them the correct change. Some students will not even touch coins when counting them, fearful that they will be confused if they move the coins or that they will forget what they have added.

Figure 4.9: When given this change, students who cannot count by twenty-fives do not start counting with the quarter, which makes the counting more difficult.

Problems counting money can be prevented or remediated by having students practice counting by twenty-fives until they have mastered it. Then you can introduce counting money, beginning with the coins of greater value and working down (rather than beginning with smaller ones). This second step of counting change beginning with larger coins may seem obvious, but habitual behavior is difficult to change. Students need to be repeatedly reminded to begin counting with quarters or half-dollars until it becomes a habit. Use the *Money Skills: Counting by Intervals* reproducibles on the CD to help students master counting change.

As students develop the habit of counting quarters first, they become adept at counting money so that when they are given the change in *Figure 4.10*, they start counting with the quarter: *$0.25 + $0.10 + $0.10 + $0.10 + $0.05 + $0.05 + $0.01 + $0.01 = $0.67*. They no longer start counting with the dimes: *$0.10 + $0.10 + $0.10 + $0.05 + $0.05 + $0.01 + $0.01 = $0.42*, getting stuck when they then have to add *$0.25*.

Figure 4.10: When students have mastered counting by twenty-fives, they can count this change with ease.

Making Change

Students with below-average math skills frequently have difficulty making change. The first problem to address is their difficulty counting money in general. But even when students can count money, they may have difficulty making change because of poor computation skills.

Because making change is usually demonstrated in word problems using subtraction, many students view making change as a task beyond their ability. They believe that they simply cannot make change because they have difficulty with subtraction.

Few students who have difficulty making change have been taught to *add* in order to make change. Students need to be explicitly taught this skill. Compare the two processes for making change illustrated in *Figure 4.11*. The student, Jodi, purchases a ball for *$0.29*, pays with a five-dollar bill, and is given four dollar-bills, two quarters, two dimes, and one penny as her change. In the first column, Jodi uses subtraction to count her change. She subtracts the cost of the ball (*$0.29*) from the money she gave the clerk (*$5.00*) in order to figure out that the change should be *$4.71*. Then she adds up her change to make sure that she has been given *$4.71*.

In the second column, Jodi uses addition to count her change. She begins with the cost of the ball (*$0.29*) and adds the change to it, beginning with the penny to make *$0.30*. Then she counts by intervals. She adds the two dimes to arrive at $0.50, adds the two quarters to make *$1.00*, and adds the four dollar-bills to bring the total to $5.00. She knows her change is correct. Making change is easy when you add instead of subtract. You can help students learn to make change using the *Money Skills: Making Change* reproducibles on the CD.

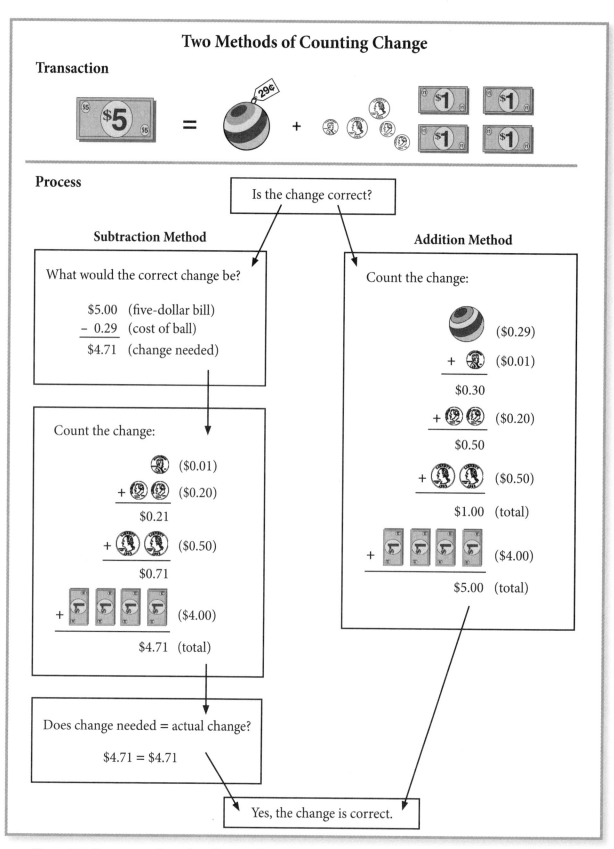

Figure 4.11: Demonstrate for students how much easier it is to use addition to count change rather than subtraction.

Odd and Even Numbers

Many students have problems with the concepts of *odd* and *even* and with identifying odd and even numbers. Students often either ignore the concepts altogether or guess when presented with a question about them.

Students who have ambiguous vocabularies do not fully understand the meaning of many common words. The word *odd* is used as *strange* or *weird*. Students with ambiguous vocabularies have difficulty understanding what is *odd* about a number. How can a number be *weird*? The concept does not make much sense, so students find *odd* and *even* incomprehensible. In Spanish, the words for *odd* and *even* are *imparada* and *parada*. They are similar to the English words *unpaired* and *paired*. But since the words *odd* and *even* do not contain common linguistic elements, students need to learn the words and concepts in a different way.

Because right/left discrimination problems make learning terms that are opposites (or have either/or relationships) difficult, many students can't remember which numbers are odd and which are even. Students who do understand the concepts of *odd* and *even* can still have difficulty determining whether numbers above *10* are odd or even.

One way to help students remember odd and even numbers is to expand their understanding of the word *odd*. Explain *even* as a pair, and the numbers that are not pairs as *odd*. Use a picture similar to *Figure 4.12* and explain:

> If you have one pair of shoes and an extra or *odd* one (a shoe without a partner), then you have *three* shoes: an *odd* number.

When students understand the concept of *odd* as *not part of a pair*, they are no longer confused by it. Provide practice with the *Odd* or *Even* reproducibles on the CD.

Figure 4.12: Students often better understand odd when they are shown that it means without a partner.

Using Weighted Learning

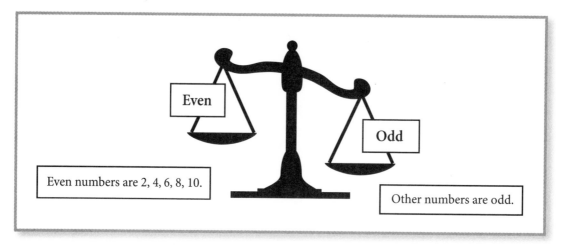

Figure 4.13: Use weighted learning to teach the concept of *even*.

Weighted learning (introduced in Chapter 2, *Right/Left Discrimination, Remediations*) helps students to remember odd and even numbers. The technique is straightforward. By "weighting" one side of an either/or relationship, you help students distinguish between the two sides. When teaching *odd* and *even* using weighted learning, you "weight" the even numbers. You teach *only* the even numbers *2, 4, 6, 8,* and *10* (as in *Figure 4.13*) and then teach students that all the other numbers are odd.

Numbers Above 10

Students who have problems discerning odd and even numbers above *10* need a way to eliminate the confusion caused by the either/or relationship. You can teach students who are right-handed to refer to the digit on the right side of the number (e.g., *127*) when determining if it is odd or even. Left-handed students need another way to remember to refer to the right digit. But remember, students with either/or confusion have difficulty discerning right from left, so addressing right/left confusion may be the first step.

Place Value and Large Numbers

Five-step process. Many students are not able to read large numbers and do not understand place values. For students who have language challenges, just remembering the *words* associated with place value can be difficult. They often become overwhelmed by the names of place values and which name goes with which digit. So, teaching the pattern of place value is an important precursor to teaching students to read large numbers. Use the following **five-step process** and the *Reading Large Numbers and Place Value* reproducibles on the CD to teach your students place value patterns and how to read numbers above *1,000*.

Step 1. Point out the repeating pattern HTO:
Hundred, Ten, One.

Step 2. Have students orally repeat the pattern until it becomes automatic:

H   T   O,   H   T   O,   H   T   O,   H   T   O,   H   T   O

Hundred Ten One, Hundred Ten One, Hundred Ten One, Hundred Ten One, Hundred Ten One

Step 3. Point out that the commas between the HTO sets correspond to the commas in numbers:

Hundred Ten One, Hundred Ten One, Hundred Ten One, Hundred Ten One, Hundred Ten One

T	B	M	Th
Trillion	Billion	Million	Thousand

5 6 5 , 2 2 4 , 9 1 4 , 3 8 7 , 2 2 6

T   B   M   Th

Step 4. On the board, draw the diagram in *Figure 4.14*. Beginning at the top right, demonstrate how easy it is to read large numbers following the *HTO* pattern: *1; 21; 321; 4,321*; and so forth, all the way to *4,321,987,654,321*. As students read each number, the rhythm of the repeating pattern becomes ingrained. Provide students who have problems reading large numbers with practice reading in this systematic way until they have mastered it, then have them practice reading random numbers.

```
                                                            1
                                                    2       1
                                            3       2       1
                                    4,      3       2       1
                            5,      4,      3       2       1
                    6       5,      4,      3       2       1
            7,      6       5,      4,      3       2       1
    8       7,      6       5,      4,      3       2       1
9       8       7,      6       5,      4,      3       2       1
1,      9       8       7,      6       5,      4,      3       2       1
2       1,      9       8       7,      6       5,      4,      3       2       1
4   3   2   1,      9       8       7,      6       5,      4,      3       2       1
```

Figure 4.14: Illustration 3.18 from page 43.

Step 5. Students now can identify any place value using the *HTO* pattern and the commas that separate each set. When students need to identify the ten-billion place, they point to the middle digit (the *T* in the *HTO* pattern) in the billion set, to the left of the billion comma. To identify the hundred-thousand place, students point to the third digit in the set, left of the thousand comma. Use the reproducibles on the CD for more practice.

Mnemonic clues. Give students **mnemonic clues**, like the ones that follow, to help them remember what the letters under the commas stand for:

A person who owns a **h**ome is a "**t**housandaire." The first comma represents *thousand*.

A person who owns a **m**ansion is a **m**illionaire. The second comma represents *million*.

If you are **B**ill Gates, you are a **b**illionaire. The third comma represents *billion*.

Billionaire begins with *bi* (like *bicycle*, i.e., two wheels) and *trillion* begins with *tri* (like *tricycle*, i.e., three wheels), so the fourth comma represents *trillion*. A *quad* has four wheels, so the fifth comma represents *quadrillion*.

Students who learn to read and write large numbers feel encouraged and are often motivated to learn more because the task is simple and the results are impressive.

Rounding Numbers

Students may be able to complete assignments and pass tests on rounding numbers even when they don't grasp the concept. They simply mimic what you've modeled without understanding. When the test is over, rounding is still a mystery. Students especially have difficulty rounding off numbers if they do not understand the concept of estimation. The difficulty is often caused by either/or confusion (see Chapter 2, *Right/Left Discrimination*): Either the number goes up or it goes down. I change *either* this number or the other number.

Some students make errors when rounding because they cannot remember what to do with the *5* (e.g., they ask "Do I round the *5* up to *6* or down to *4*?"). Students who do not understand place value also often have difficulty rounding. It is like not being able to see the forest for the trees. They may be confused by the vocabulary of place values and may not be able to determine which number to round (forest) because they are so focused on the operation (trees) of whether to change the number or leave it unchanged.

Give students ample practice in rounding using the progressive exercises provided in the *Rounding Numbers* reproducibles on the CD. It may seem too easy, but students really should start by rounding numbers that end in *9* or *1* (e.g., *59* and *21*). When correctly rounding these numbers becomes automatic, introduce numbers ending in *8* and *2*, and so on. Keep adding numbers until students are taught that the number that ends with *5* is rounded up (See *Rounding Exercises: Numbers 9, 8, 7, 6, 5, 4, 3, 2, and 1* on the CD). Sometimes the visual clue illustrated by *Figure 4.15* helps students remember to round up the number *5*.

Figure 4.15: Help students remember to round up the number 5 with this visual clue.

Symbols (Mathematical)

Students have many difficulties with symbols: not paying attention to symbols in equations, confusing symbols that are similar (such as − and ÷), and forgetting meanings of symbols that are not used frequently. But some students have much more difficulty with symbols. Students with right/left discrimination problems often find symbols confusing, and students whose minds race make frequent symbol-related errors.

Students may overlook the basic symbols for addition (+), subtraction (−), and multiplication (x) or make assumptions when they are completing work too quickly or without sufficient attention. These kinds of errors happen more frequently for students with racing minds. Have students bold the symbols before beginning to solve problems in order to focus their attention on the operation.

The symbols most often recognized as causing confusion are the symbols for *greater than* (>) and *less than* (<). This concept/symbol combination constitutes a double either/or relationship: *Either* the number is higher *or* lower than another, and *either* > *or* < represents *more than*. You can help students differentiate between these symbols using weighted learning and mnemonic clues.

The symbols for inches and feet are another example of common either/or confusion. The inch mark (") is two marks while the foot mark (') is one. Logically the smaller measurement would be represented by the single mark (') and the larger by the double mark ("), but the reverse is true. To help students deal with this inversion, give them a mnemonic clue. Have them think of the foot mark as being longer than the inch mark as in *Figure 4.16*.

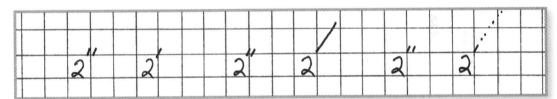

Figure 4.16: To help students remember that feet are longer than inches, show them how to draw long foot-marks and short inch-marks.

The multiple symbols used to indicate multiplication and division (as in *Figure 4.17*) confuse many students. Help students create a bookmark to use as a quick reference to all the multiplication and division symbols. Over time, confusion will fade as students continually identify the symbols correctly. You may also find helpful the key provided in the Mathematical Symbols reproducibles on the CD.

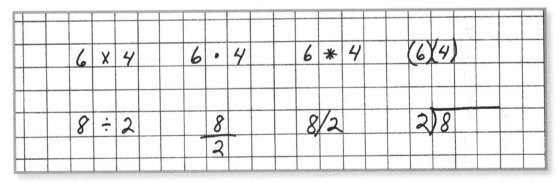

Figure 4.17: A bookmark that shows all the symbols of multiplication and division is an easy reference for students.

The equal symbol (=) is often misunderstood by students with poor math skills. They may believe that = means "the answer is" rather than "the same as." This underdeveloped understanding of the symbol and concept is acceptable in young students, but it presents a problem for students in higher grades because it limits their understanding of equations. Correct misunderstandings early on by explicitly teaching the meanings of the symbols.

Two more symbols that cause confusion are the percentage sign (%) and pi (π). The percentage sign sometimes means "sale" to students and π is sometimes taken to mean, literally, a *pie* because it is used with circles.

Display mathematical symbols in the classroom on posters and mobiles to eliminate confusion. Make bookmarks for students showing the symbols they find problematic. Bookmarks may be different for each student, depending on the symbols they find confusing. Having one bookmark that shows all the symbols may be confusing for students, so it is best to individualize them. For most students who have weak math skills, one bookmark that shows just a few symbols is most helpful. As those symbols are mastered, make another bookmark with new symbols for students to learn. Provide practice with the *Mathematical Symbols* reproducibles on the CD.

Telling Time

Figure 4.18: Students who have no problem telling time with a digital clock can be challenged by a traditional clock face.

Fractions of an Hour

Students usually do not have difficulty telling time with digital clocks or watches (as in *Figure 4.18*), but may not be able to tell time using traditional timepieces. Digital timepieces are one-dimensional. They only display the hour and minute (and sometimes the seconds), so they are easy to read. Traditional clocks are two-dimensional. They use a visual-spatial relationship between the minutes and hours (and the seconds as well on some clocks). Students may be able to read *1:02* on a digital clock and know what time it is, but they may have no concept of how *1:02* relates to the rest of the minutes in the hour, to the previous hour, or to the next hour. When they hear terms like *half past, a quarter to, a quarter after*, and *five to the hour*, they do not know what they mean. Consequently, it is not unusual for students who do not understand how to read traditional timepieces to think that there are 25 minutes in a quarter of an hour (equating it with 25 cents in a quarter of a dollar). These students have difficulty planning and using time. As they get older the information gap in their understanding of time interferes with their ability to function effectively in everyday activities.

Students who do not learn to tell time with traditional clocks often lack basic information about the nature of time. They do not fully understand that there are two sets of numbers represented on a clock face: *hours* and *minutes*. If a clock face has Arabic numbers (clocks with Roman numerals are even more confusing for students), students can usually grasp the concept of twelve hours. But, because of the inversion inherent in traditional clocks, students do not understand how to read the hours. The inversion is that the larger unit, the hour, is identified by the smaller hand of the clock, while the smaller unit, the minute, is identified by the larger hand.

Even more problematic for students is the fact that many clocks do not show numbers for the 60 minutes. Some clocks have lines that represent the minutes, but some do not. Some clocks indicate the minutes in five-minute intervals; however, these indications are located near the numbers representing hours. Clocks designed to teach students do indicate the minutes with numbers, but since few students need clocks that detail all 60 minutes to learn to tell time, these clocks are not readily available. As a result, students grow up without ever learning to tell time and understand time using a traditional clock.

The clock faces in *Figures 4.19*, *Figures 4.20a–4.20b*, and *Figures 4.21a–4.21c* (and the corresponding reproducibles on the CD) are designed to help students understand and learn time concepts. You can use the clock face in *Figure 4.19* in two ways:

1. Have students point to the hours and minutes on the clock face. Say the time and have students point to the hour and minute. For example, ask students to show you *1:25* on the clock face. They should point to the large *1* in the inner circle of numbers and to the small *25* on the outer circle. At this time, don't discuss the concept of the small hand being between the hour numbers unless students inquire about it. During this first stage of instruction, it is not necessary to explain that the hour hand gradually moves to the next hour. You can explain this concept later. Complete clock reading exercises daily until students can easily point to the correct time.

2. Have students practice reading digital clock times and converting the time to the traditional clock face display. Use the reproducibles on the CD, provide a written list of digital clock times, or prompt students by giving the times orally. Have students point to the hours and minutes on the clock face or have them draw in the hands on the clock face. Repeat the exercise until students can identify the hours and minutes correctly.

The clock face in *Figure 4.19* indicates all 60 minutes. The minutes shown on the clock faces in *Figures 4.20a* and *4.20b* and in *Figures 4.21a, 4.21b*, and *4.21c* are gradually reduced in stages. *Figure 4.20a* shows even-numbered minutes. *Figure 4.20b* shows the odd-numbered minutes. *Figures 4.21a, 4.21b*, and *4.21c* indicate the minutes in intervals of three, of four, and of five (respectively). Use these clock faces to gradually reduce students' need to see the minute numbers on the clock face.

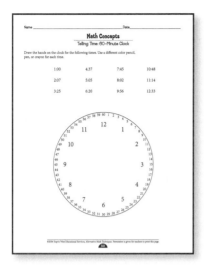

Figure 4.19: Have students practice telling time on a traditional clock face using the 60-Minute Clock reproducible.

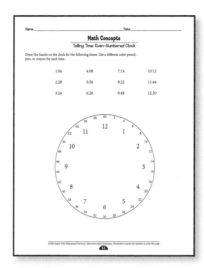

Figure 4.20a: Use the Even-Numbered Clock reproducible to transition students from reading clocks that indicate all 60 minutes.

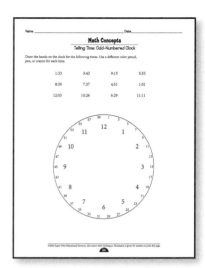

Figure 4.20b: Continue to reduce students' reliance on minute numbers using the Odd-Numbered Clock reproducible.

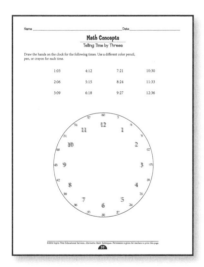

Figure 4.21a: The clock face in the Telling Time by Threes reproducible indicates minutes in intervals of three.

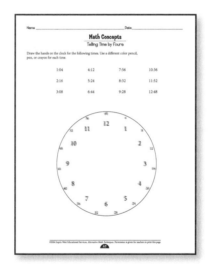

Figure 4.21b: The clock face in the Telling Time by Fours reproducible indicates minutes in intervals of four.

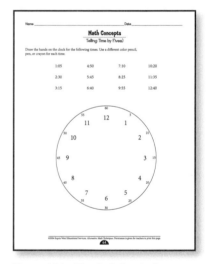

Figure 4.21c: The clock face in the Telling Time by Fives reproducible indicates minutes in intervals of five.

As soon as students can easily identify the time on a clock face without the minute numbers, introduce the concept of the small hand moving gradually to the next hour. Make small marks (or have students make marks) halfway between all of the large, inner-circle numbers to indicate the half hours as in *Figure 4.22*. Instruct students to draw the small hand pointing to the hour of the lesser number if the minutes are less than 30, pointing to the half mark if the minutes equal 30, and somewhere past the half mark if the minutes are more than 30.

Once students understand the concept that the small hand moves gradually to the next hour and can correctly position the hour and minute hands, make two more marks between each of the large numbers of the inner circle to represent quarters of an hour (as in *Figure 4.22*). Then have students draw the small hand between the smaller number and the first mark for minutes less than *15*, between this mark and the middle mark for minutes between *15* and *30*, between the middle mark and the third mark for minutes between 30 and 45, and between the third mark and the next number for minutes between *45* and *60*. Label the marks *1/4, 1/2,* and *3/4*. Then introduce and practice the concept of fractions of an hour.

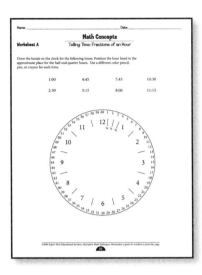

Figure 4.22: Using the Telling Time: Fractions of an Hour reproducible, have students make marks between the large numbers on the clock face to indicate the half hours and quarter hours.

Using the reproducibles, students gradually move from reading time on these clock faces to reading time on traditional clocks that do not have minute numbers or marks. Once students can identify the hours and minutes using the clock faces in the reproducibles, they can begin to practice moving the hour hand. Some students find out on their own that the hour hand does not continue to point to the hour. Other students have to be taught this concept. You can use the same reproducibles on the CD to teach students that the hour hand moves.

When teaching this skill, build on previously acquired time-telling skills. For example, teach that the hour hand points to the hour until the minutes pass the half-hour mark (30 minutes). When students master this concept, teach them where the hour hand points for the quarter hours. Be sure to also refer to a real clock to help students understand how the hour hand moves.

The *Telling Time* reproducibles shown in *Figures 4.23–4.29*) can help you clear up misunderstandings about **fractions of an hour.** Students who do not fully understand fractions can usually divide the clock (the whole) in half and divide again to make quarters. But students often become confused when they divide the clock again and find that eighths of an hour (7 1/2 or 7.5 minutes) are not whole numbers. Clocks are not pizzas, and students' understanding of fractions of an hour usually ends here.

Students who have difficulty with fractions of an hour need to continually return to the fractions presented in *Figures 4.23–4.29* until they know the number of minutes for each fraction and can recall them automatically.

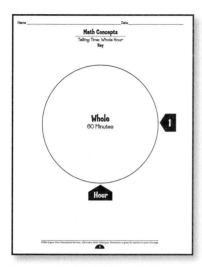

Figure 4.23: The Telling Time: Whole Hour reproducible helps students understand an hour as a whole.

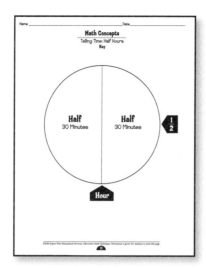

Figure 4.24: The Telling Time: Half Hours reproducible helps students understand the concept of a half hour.

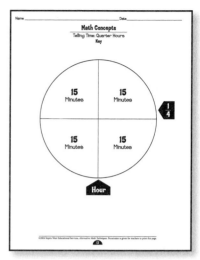

Figure 4.25: The Telling Time: Quarter Hours reproducible helps students understand quarter hours.

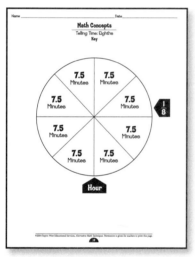

Figure 4.26: The Telling Time: Eighths reproducible shows that 1/8 of an hour is 7.5 minutes.

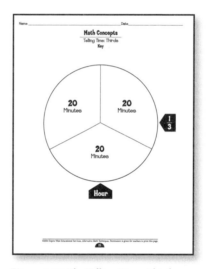

Figure 4.27: The Telling Time: Thirds illustrates 1/3 of an hour (or 20 minutes).

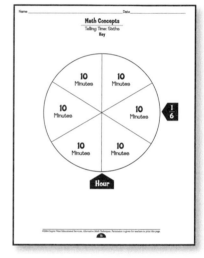

Figure 4.28: The Telling Time: Sixths helps students understand that 1/6 of an hour is the same as 10 minutes.

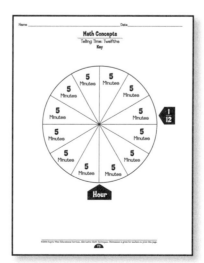

Figure 4.29: The Telling Time: Twelfths shows that 1/12 of an hour = 5 minutes.

The Language of Time

Time Zones

A fifteen-year-old student, Yvette, did not understand time zones. Yvette had seen pictures of the earth from space, so her visual concept was correctly that the earth was round. She described the earth as a sphere or globe. Yvette's quantitative concept of the earth, however, was flat: She believed it was the same time everywhere on earth. Yvette heard that students on the East Coast of the United States needed to phone students on the West Coast three hours later but did not understand why.

It was not enough to explain to Yvette how the earth rotates to produce day and night. I used illustrations, a lamp, and a globe to demonstrate the earth's rotation and repeated the explanation and demonstration over several weeks. Yvette then began to understand how day and night occur—and the concept of time zones.

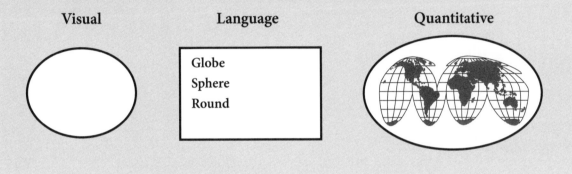

Visual	Language	Quantitative
	Globe Sphere Round	

Students can find time terms difficult to understand, including:

- *a.m.* and *p.m.*
- *Dawn* and *dusk*
- *Daybreak* and *nightfall*
- *Midnight* and *midday*
- *Morning, afternoon*, and *evening*
- *Sunrise* and *sunset*

The *Time Language* reproducibles and the *Day/Night Planner* on the CD (see Figure 4.30) can help students understand the concept of a 24-hour day and how to use the language of time. Every day have students fill in the *Day/Night Planner* with their activities in as much detail as is age-appropriate. Encourage them to use the words that refer to parts of the day when they talk about the times of the day or night that they have planned. For example, students may refer to having breakfast at *dawn* or doing their homework after *sunset*. Have students fill out the *Day/Night Planner* and discuss their plans daily until the concepts and vocabulary are mastered.

Figure 4.30: Have students fill in the Day/Night Planner every day.

Word Problems

Students who have poor math skills usually report that they hate word problems. They struggle to understand the problems and frequently get them wrong on assignments and tests. There are four learning differences that can make word problems especially difficult for students:

1. **Reading challenges.** Students who have reading challenges struggle to read the problems in the first place. Some may be able to read the words adequately but, because of underdeveloped or ambiguous vocabularies, are not able to fully comprehend word problems. Students who have **underdeveloped**

vocabularies do not know many words that their peers know. Students who have **ambiguous** vocabularies have an imprecise understanding of many words.

2. **Nonsequential thinking.** Some students follow a nonsequential logic in which they see connections that other students do not (as in the sidebar *On a Personal Note: Thinking Differently About Word Problems*).

3. **Racing minds.** Students with racing minds may be triggered to go off on a tangent or to do opposite operations.

4. **Difficulties with right/left discrimination.** Students often read too much into word problems. They find it difficult to decide which operation to use or which to do first.

Three Techniques

Use the three techniques that follow to help students with these challenges to solve word problems. These techniques usually take a long time to develop but are highly effective once in place.

1. **Write word problems.** Have students write word problems systematically and regularly (see *Figure 4.31*). **Systematically** means setting up a system for students to write word problems that reflect the day's lesson or that are about one specific object, using each operation of addition, subtraction, multiplication, and division. **Regularly** means every day or at least twice a week. Ideally students write one or more word problems every day. This provides the needed intensity to become familiar with the language of word problems and proficient with the operations. As skill level increases, students can add extraneous numbers to the word problems or write multiple-step problems. This technique takes a long time to produce results, but if students have a system and use it regularly, they will master word problems. You can also provide students with objects and have them write word problems, or use the *Writing Word Problems* reproducibles on the CD.

2. **Drawing word problems.** This technique can be used in conjunction with writing word problems. Students do not have to have artistic ability to draw word problems. The objects can be represented by squares or circles, and people by stick figures. Drawing objects in various locations on the page can show operations; for example, grouped objects represent addition or multiplication. Separated objects represent subtraction or division. Students may think this process is time consuming or unnecessary, but if they get in the habit of drawing word problems, they are better able to visualize them and make sense of even the most complex ones. Provide practice with the *Drawing Word Problems* reproducibles on the CD.

Word Problem Prompt

"I see that there are 14 boys in the class and 16 girls, so in my word problem I'm going to ask how many students there are all together. Now you write a word problem. Look around the room and choose two types of things you want to add together."

Figure 4.31: Model how to write an original word problem, then have students write their own.

3. Use memory clues. Show students how to use memory clues to remember the steps for solving word problems. For example, post the steps for solving problems (see *Figure 4.32*) in the classroom or print them on a bookmark so that students can refer to them until they commit them to memory. You can post each step in a different location in the classroom. For example, post Step 1 in the left corner of the front of the classroom, Step 2 in the center of the front of the classroom, Step 3 in the right corner, Step 4 in the center of the right wall, and Step 5 in the back corner of the right wall. The physical space between each posted step provides a sense of separation for each step. Another place to post the steps is on the floor. Some students find it easier to learn steps by walking to them as they memorize them.

Five Steps for Solving Word Problems

1. Determine what I need to find.

2. Decide what information I need in order to find it.

3. Decide which arithmetic operation I need to use.

4. Do the math.

5. Check my work to see if it agrees with the first step.

Figure 4.32: As a memory clue, post the steps for solving word problems in your classroom.

Teaching Addition

When students count in order to solve addition problems, they are not really adding. They are sequencing rather than grouping numbers. Not only is counting time consuming, it limits one's ability to learn higher math because it requires so much effort. The goal for all students is automatic recall (see Chapter 3, The Hierarchy of Number-Fact Skills), but this is not easily obtained or possible for some students, especially those with learning problems.

There is more to addition than memorizing the number facts. Adding is the grouping of numbers (single digits, numbers with multiple digits, and columns of numbers) and includes operations like carrying and regrouping. The same thought processes that make learning number facts difficult make the learning of addition concepts and operations problematic.

Number Patterns

Students learn many number patterns at an early age; for example, to count by twos, fives, and tens. As students learn more math, they may see the pattern in the progression of fractions: *1/2, 1/4, 1/8, 1/16, 1/32, 1/64*, etc. However, not all students see patterns, and many don't learn on their own to use patterns to understand and complete math operations. They need to be taught about patterns. Once students learn patterns and know how to use them, they often grasp the underlying concepts.

Odd and Even Patterns

Teach students to remember addition and subtraction number facts using the concepts of *odd* and *even*:

1. The combination of two even numbers always results in an even number.

2. The combination of two odd numbers always results in an even number.

3. The combination of an odd and an even number always results in an odd number.

Figure 5.1a illustrates these three odd and even patterns in addition and subtraction. These facts help students later in the multiplication of signed numbers (*Figure 5.1b*). Use the *Number Patterns: Odd* and *Even* reproducibles on the CD to provide practice.

E O O E	+ − + −
E O E O	+ − − +
+ or − E E O O	× + + − −

Figure 5.1a: Illustrating odd- and even-number pattern in this way helps students remember them.

Figure 5.1b: The odd- and even-number pattern is similar to the pattern of the multiplication of positive and negative numbers.

Numbers in Numbers

One of the first things to teach students who do not know addition facts is the pattern of numbers in numbers. For example, teach students that *4* is made up of four 1s, two *2s*, one *3* and one *1*, or one *2* and two *1s* (as detailed in *Figure 5.2*). Encourage students to explore number combinations. Use *Figures 5.3a–5.3e* and the *Numbers in Numbers* reproducibles to assist them. For some, this exploration will lead to mastery of the number facts with automatic recall. For others, it will lead to an understanding of number relationships and reduce the need for counting.

Figure 5.2: The number combinations of 2, 3, and 4.

```
2 = 1         3 = 2  1       4 = 3   2   2   1
    1             1  1           1   2   1   1
                     1                   1   1
                                             1
```

Figure 5.3a: The number combinations of 5.

```
5 = 4   3   2   2   3   1
    1   2   2   1   1   1
            1   1   1   1
                    1   1
                        1
```

Figure 5.3b: The number combinations of 6.

```
6 = 5   4   4   3   3   3   2   2   2   1
    1   2   1   3   2   1   2   2   1   1
            1       1   1   2   1   1   1
                        1       1   1   1
                                    1   1
                                        1
```

Figure 5.3c: The number combinations of 7.

```
7 = 6   5   5   4   4   4   3   3   3   3   2   2   2   1
    1   2   1   3   2   1   3   2   2   1   2   2   1   1
            1       1   1       1   2   1   2   2   1   1
                        1           1   1   1   2   1   1
                                            1   1   1   1
                                                1   1   1
                                                    1   1
                                                        1
```

Figure 5.3d: The number combinations of 8.

```
8 = 7  6  6  5  5  5  4  4  4  4  4  3  3  3  3  3  2  2  2  2  1
    1  2  1  3  2  1  4  3  2  2  1  3  3  2  2  1  2  2  2  1  1
          1     1  1        1  2  1     1  2  1  2  1  1  2  2  1  1  1
             1                 1  1        1  1  1  1  2  1  1  1  1
                            1                 1  1     1  1  1  1
                                              1           1  1  1
                                                          1  1
                                                             1
```

Figure 5.3e: The number combinations of 9.

```
9 = 8  7  7  6  6  6  5  5  5  5  5  4  4  4  4  4  4  3  3  3  3  3  3  2  2  2  2  1
    1  2  1  3  2  1  4  3  2  2  1  4  3  3  2  2  1  3  3  2  2  2  1  2  2  2  1  1
          1     1  1        1  2  1  1  1  2  1  2  1  1  3  2  2  2  1  1  2  2  1  1  1
             1                 1  1  1  1  1  1  1     1  2  1  1  1  2  1  1  1  1
                            1                 1  1  1     1  1  1  1  1  1  1  1  1
                                              1              1  1     1  1  1  1
                                                             1           1  1  1
                                                                         1  1
                                                                            1
```

Addition Patterns

Show students all of the single-digit number facts together (using the *Number-Fact Patterns* reproducibles on the CD). The patterns in these 81 facts are uncanny. Some students see the patterns immediately, but you will have to point out patterns for some students. Once they are introduced to the patterns, many students use them to remember the number facts. In *Figures 5.4a–5.4c*, note the following patterns:

Pattern 1: *Figure 5.4a*. Point out that horizontally and vertically the sums of the number facts increase by one. (See shaded area.)

Pattern 2: *Figure 5.4b*. Have students look at the patterns of the shaded diagonals, top left to bottom right. When adding two of the same number (*e.g.*, 5 + 5) the answer always equals an even number. Introduce the concept of doubling the number if it is not already understood.

Pattern 3: *Figure 5.4b*. Looking at the diagonals on either side of Pattern 2, and going in the same direction, point out that the sum of the numbers increases by two.

Pattern 4: *Figure 5.4b*. The diagonal column in the middle is even and the shaded columns to both sides of it are odd.

Pattern 5: *Figure 5.4c*. Have students look at the diagonal from top right to bottom left. The sum of the numbers is the same for each fact in this diagonal.

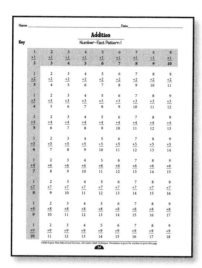

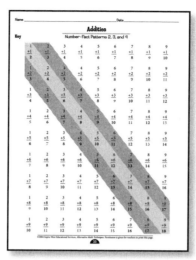

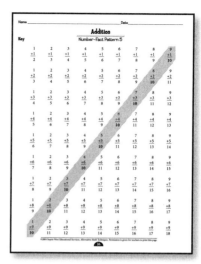

Figure 5.4a: The Number-Fact Pattern 1 reproducible shows how sums increase by one both horizontally and vertically.

Figure 5.4b: The Number-Fact Patterns 2, 3, and 4 reproducibles shows one even-numbered and two odd-numbered patterns that increase by two.

Figure 5.4c: The Number-Fact Pattern 5 reproducible shows the repeating pattern of sums.

Use Number-Fact Pattern 6 (*Figure 5.5*) to help students identify the number facts they know and do not know. Show them that there are only 45 addition facts to learn and that they may already know many of them: The number facts in the gray shaded area are the same as their opposites in the unshaded area. They are the same numbers upside down (e.g., *2 + 1 = 3 and 1 + 2 = 3*). Once unknown facts are identified, teach them using the techniques that follow. Use the *Number Patterns: Addition Facts* reproducibles on the CD to provide practice.

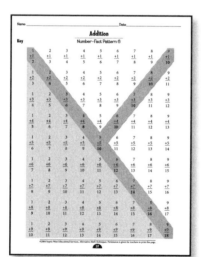

Figure 5.5: Use the Number-Fact Pattern 6 reproducible to demonstrate that there are only 45 addition facts students need to learn.

Note: Assess students' knowledge of number facts over the course of a few days. If all the number facts are tested in one sitting, most students will be able to use their knowledge of some facts to remember others. When you assess over time, students' usual way of recalling or calculating the facts becomes evident.

45 Addition Facts

When students know the multiplication facts but count when doing addition and subtraction, I ask, "How many multiplication facts or times tables are there?" Students usually reply that there are nine or twelve times tables.

I then ask, "How many addition facts are there?" The usual response is "I don't know," so I give some choices: "about a hundred, a thousand, a million, or an infinite number?" Students typically respond that there are either a million or an infinite number of addition facts.

This explains why students count the addition and subtraction facts but know the multiplication facts by automatic recall. They have never learned that there are only 45 addition facts! When working with students who already know the multiplication facts by automatic recall, you can usually remediate the addition facts in just a couple of days or weeks by isolating the ones they don't know and helping them memorize them. When students know the addition facts by automatic recall, they no longer need to count or guess when doing addition and subtraction. (Students who do not know the multiplication facts by automatic recall may not be able to learn the addition facts as quickly.)

Sequencing-to-the-Right-and-Back Pattern

The number facts that add to *10* are important to know by automatic recall because they can be used as **number keys** (number facts that can be used as reference points for other number facts) and in some subtraction problems. The pattern that follows can be of great help to students who are struggling with the number facts that add to *10*. Use the pattern, along with the *Number Patterns: Sequencing to the Right and Back* reproducibles on the CD, to provide practice.

The mnemonic clue, or pattern, in *Figures 5.6a–5.6c* helps students remember the number facts that add up to *10*. Using this pattern, students always get the facts correct and often learn to automatically recall them. Even if the facts don't become automatic for students, they can still use the pattern.

To teach students the pattern, follow these steps:

1. Have students write as they say, "one, two, three, four, five" (*Figure 5.6a*).

2. Then have students write as they say, "five and five are ten" (*Figure 5.6b*).

3. Then, beginning under the four and moving from right to left, have students continue to write as they say, "six, seven, eight, and nine" (*Figure 5.6c*). Each of the five number combinations equals *10*.

The more that students use this pattern for sequencing to the right and back, always getting the number facts correct when doing calculations, the quicker the number facts become automatic.

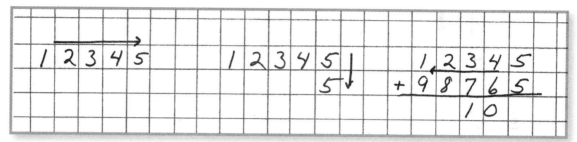

Figure 5.6a: Students begin the sequence-to-the-right-and-back pattern by writing 1–5.

Figure 5.6b: Students continue the sequence-to-the-right-and-back pattern, beginning with 5 + 5.

Figure 5.6c: By filling in the rest of the numbers sequentially, students complete the sequence-to-the-right-and-back pattern.

The "One Up, One Down" Pattern

Another pattern that helps students remember the number facts that add up to *10* is called "one up, one down." Sometimes just seeing this pattern (see *Figure 5.7*) enables students to remember the number facts. Other times, students need to practice writing the pattern to learn the facts.

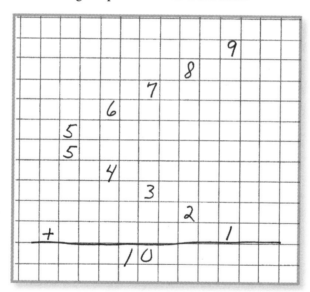

Figure 5.7: The visual "one up, one down" pattern helps many students, but not as many as the "five and five" pattern.

Patterns for Adding to 9

Use the following three methods and the *Number Patterns: Adding to 9* reproducibles on the CD to help students recall the facts for adding numbers to 9.

1. Using 10 as a base. The pattern in *Figure 5.8* uses *10* as a base. Teach students that, when they need to add 9 to any number, they can first add *1* to the *9* to get *10*. Have them add the number to the *10*, to get a total, and then subtract 1 for their answer. For example, when solving *9 + 6 =*, the 9 becomes *10*: *10 + 6 = 16*. Then you subtract the *1* from the total: *16 – 1 = 15*, so *9 + 6 = 15*. Another example is *9 + 4*. The 9 becomes *10*: *10 + 4 = 14*. *14 – 1 = 13*, so *9 + 4 = 13*.

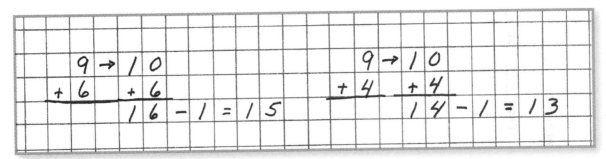

Figure 5.8: Teach students to change the 9 to a 10, then subtract 1 to get the answer.

2. **Using number keys of doubles.** Another pattern that helps students add numbers to 9 is to use a number key (see *Number Key Patterns* in the section that follows). In *Figure 5.9*, students use the number keys of doubles (e.g., *9 + 9 = 18*) as a base to find the answer. *9 + 7* is the same as *9 + 9 – 2*. And *9 + 8* is the same as *8 + 8 + 1*.

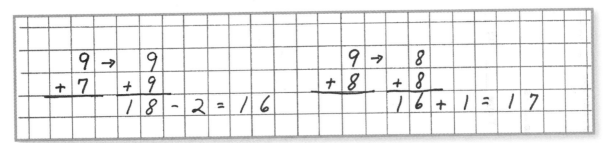

Figure 5.9: Show students how to use the number keys of doubles to solve equations when adding numbers to 9.

3. **Using numbers "teened."** This technique for adding numbers to 9 is quicker to use than the first two. It requires fewer steps, and many students find it easy to remember. Teach students:

   9 + any number = 1 less than that number "teened."

So when adding *9 + 5* (as in *Figure 5.10*), students focus on the *5*, subtract one to get *4*, and then add the suffix *-teen* to make *14*. For *9 + 6*, students reduce 6 to 5 and add *-teen* to get *15*: *9 + 6 = 15*.

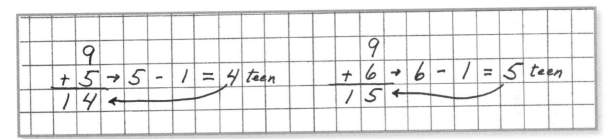

Figure 5.10: When adding numbers to 9, students subtract one from the number and add *–teen* to get their answer.

Number Key Patterns

The numbers that add up to *10* and the numbers doubled (e.g., *2 + 2*) are **number keys**. When students know these keys, they can unlock the rest of the number facts using number relationships.

Number keys of doubles. When students know the number keys, they can easily learn to add or subtract one from them to recall the number facts. In this way they learn to use number relationships. Once they have mastered adding and subtracting one from the number keys, they learn to add and subtract two. *Figure 5.11* is an example of a number key pattern. Using the *Number Patterns: Number Keys* reproducibles on the CD, have students practice using number keys until they quickly and easily remember the patterns and can use the number relationships to complete computations—or until they learn the number facts by automatic recall.

Number Key	Down one	Up one		Number Key	Down one	Up one
5 +5 = 10	5 +4 = 9	5 +6 = 11		6 +6 = 12	6 +5 = 11	6 +7 = 13
7 +7 = 14	7 +6 = 13	7 +8 = 15		8 +8 = 16	8 +7 = 15	8 +9 = 17

Figure 5.11: Students see the pattern in the number keys of doubles +/– 1.

Number keys of 10. After students have learned to use the number keys up and down one (+/– 1), show them how to start with the number keys and go up and down by two, as in *Figure 5.12*. When students have mastered using the double number keys, teach them to use the number keys that add up to ten in the same pattern (see *Figure 5.13*).

Number Key	Down two	Up two		Number Key	Down two	Up two
5 +5 = 10	5 +3 = 8	5 +7 = 12		6 +6 = 12	6 +4 = 10	6 +8 = 14
7 +7 = 14	7 +5 = 12	7 +9 = 16		8 +8 = 16	8 +6 = 14	8 +10 = 18

Figure 5.12: Students see the patterns in the number keys of doubles +/– 2.

Add to Ten

9	9	9		8	8	8
+1	+0	+2		+2	+1	+3
10	9	11		10	9	11

7	7	7		8	8	8
+3	+2	+4		+4	+3	+5
10	9	11		10	9	11

Figure 5.13: Students see the patterns in the number keys that add up to 10, +/−1.

More Number-Fact Patterns

The pattern students use to learn or remember number facts that add up to ten can be used to learn and remember other number facts. Besides providing practice with number facts, these patterns can be fun to create. The following examples demonstrate the patterns that add to numbers *11* to *16*, but students can use the same patterns to explore the numbers that add up to *20, 25, 49, 100,* and, in fact, any number. Playing with these patterns enable students who otherwise avoid math to practice. They show them to their parents, siblings, and friends. Every time they demonstrate the pattern, they practice the number facts. Use the *More Number-Fact Patterns* reproducibles on the CD to provide further practice.

Using the Sequence-to-the-Right-and-Back Pattern for Even Numbers

You can use the sequence-to-the-right-and-back pattern to help students learn other number facts and to explore number relationships. *Figure 5.14* shows how to use the pattern to add up to *12*:

1. Have students write the numbers as they say, "one, two, three, four, five, six" (*Figure 5.14a*).

2. As they say "six and six are twelve," they write another *6* beneath the *6* (*Figure 5.14b*).

3. Then, beginning under the *5*, students write from right to left as they say, "seven, eight, nine, ten, and eleven." Each of the six number combinations equals *12* (*Figure 5.14c*).

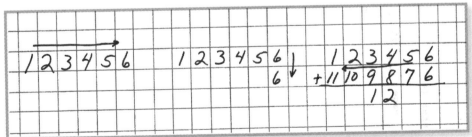

Figure 5.14a: Students apply the sequence-to-the-right-and-back pattern to 12, beginning by writing 1–6.

Figure 5.14b: Students write 6–11 from right to left on the second line.

Figure 5.14c: All six number combinations equal twelve.

Figure 5.15 shows the same pattern applied to *14*. Students write as they say, "one, two, three, four, five, six, seven." Then they write another *7* beneath the *7*: "seven and seven are fourteen." Beginning under the *6*, students write from right to left as they say, "eight, nine, ten, eleven, twelve, thirteen." All the number combinations add up to *14*. Point out to students that this pattern, which doubles the final number, always adds to an even number.

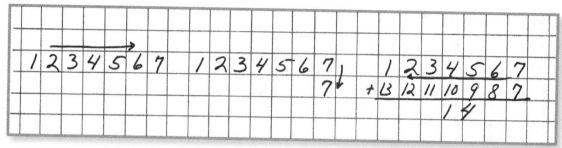

Figure 5.15: Applying the sequence-to-the-right-and-back pattern to 14.

Adjusting the Sequence-to-the-Right-and-Back Pattern for Odd Numbers

To use the sequence-to-the-right-and-back pattern to obtain an odd number, teach students to not repeat the last number in the top line beneath it, but to continue counting, as in *Figures 5.16a–5.16c*.

1. Have students write as they say, "one, two, three, four, five," (*Figure 5.16a*).

2. Then have students continue the sequence (rather than repeat the last number) and write as they say, "five and six are eleven" (*Figure 5.16b*).

3. Beginning under the *4*, have students write from right to left as they say "seven, eight, nine, and ten" (*Figure 5.16c*). All the combinations equal *11*, an odd number.

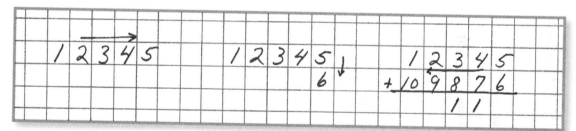

Figure 5.16a: Students learn to use the sequence-to-the-right-and-back pattern to add to 11, beginning by writing 1–5.

Figure 5.16b: Students adjust the sequence-to-the-right-and-back pattern for odd numbers by not repeating the last number on the top line.

Figure 5.16c: All five number combinations add up to 11.

Students can use the same pattern for the numbers that add to *13* (see *Figure 5.17*). Have students write as they say, "one, two, three, four, five, six." Then have them write a *7* beneath the *6* and say "six and seven are thirteen." Students continue to write (from right to left) as they say, "eight, nine, ten, eleven, and twelve." All the combinations equal *13*.

The same pattern and procedure can be used to explore the numbers that add up to other sums. For example, the pattern for numbers that add up to *15* is shown in *Figure 5.18*.

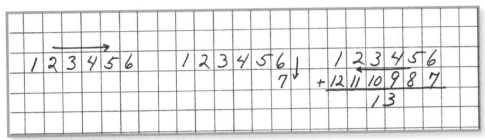

Figure 5.17: Students adjust the sequence-to-the-right-and-back pattern to add up to 13, an odd number.

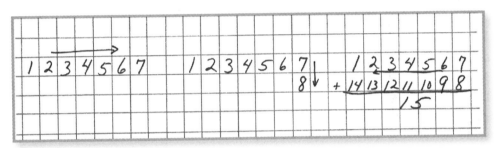

Figure 5.18: Students use the same pattern for 15.

Further Practice With Patterns

Students find the three patterns in *Figures 5.19, 5.20,* and *5.21* fun to play with. Generally, students like to play with large numbers and to show friends and family the patterns. Each time they do these computations, they practice the double-number facts, the number facts that add up to ten, and the skill of carrying.

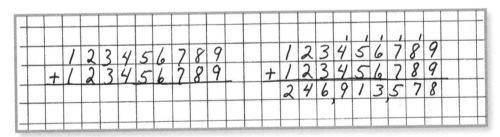

Figure 5.19: Have students practice doubling the numbers 1–9 as a multidigit challenge.

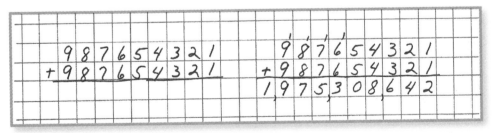

Figure 5.20: Reverse the order of numbers, so that students are practicing doubling the numbers from 9 to 1 as a multidigit challenge.

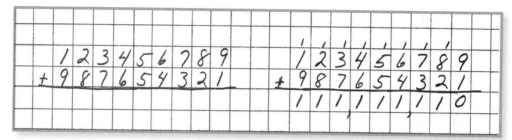

Figure 5.21: Students practice addition facts as a multidigit challenge.

Using Odd and Even Patterns to Deduce Number Facts

Students can use the odd and even patterns to deduce and check the addition and subtraction number facts (see *Odd and Even Patterns* earlier in this chapter). In *Figures 5.22a* and *5.22b*, students must solve 9 + 7 =. Since both are odd numbers, students can apply the knowledge that the combination of two odd numbers always results in an even number.

Ask students to draw a number line similar to *Figure 5.22a* (or use the one provided on the *Number Patterns: Odd and Even* reproducible on the CD). Students know that the answer must be an even number, so have them cap the odd numbers as in *Figure 5.22b*. With the odd numbers capped, or unavailable, the number line is stretched so that there is more space between possible correct answers.

Figure 5.22a: Students draw a number line.

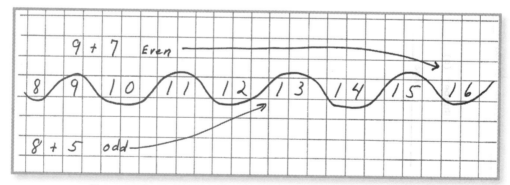

Figure 5.22b: Students cap the odd numbers; the answer can't be odd.

Students see the even numbers as possible answers and eliminate some of them using number facts. *10* and *12* are too close to *9*, so they cannot be the answers. Using number keys of doubles, students proceed: *7 + 7 = 14* and *9 + 9 = 18*, so the answer is between *14* and *18*. 15 and *17* are odd, so they are not available. Therefore, the answer must be *16*.

Let's look at another problem using the same number line, but with a total that is odd. To solve 8 + 5 =, students apply the knowledge that the combination of an odd and an even number always results in an odd number (because 8 is even and 5 is odd). Using the number line (*Figure 5.22b*) students now look at the odd numbers as possible answers, eliminating the numbers on the even side of the line. If they use number keys of doubles, they know that *8 + 8 = 16* and *5 + 5 = 10*, so the answer is between 10 and 16. That leaves *11, 13, and 15* as possible answers. At this point, some students realize that the sum is 13, but others may need to eliminate 11 and 15. They may use the number keys *8 + 2 = 10 + 1 = 11* and *8 + 8 = 16 – 1 = 15* in order to determine that the sum is *13*.

Sometimes students find it easier to understand the odd and even patterns when either the odd or the even numbers are enlarged on the number line, as in *Figure 5.23*.

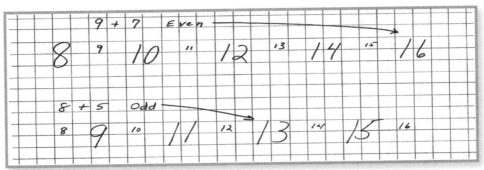

Figure 5.23: Using a number line with enlarged even or odd numbers (instead of capped numbers) is sometimes helpful for students.

Reinforcing Number Facts

Mnemonic Cues For Number Facts

Use **mnemonic cues**, like these "stories" to help students remember number facts. Try these examples:

1 + 1 = 2 eyes.

2 + 2 = 4 limbs.

3 + 3 = 6 legs on an insect.

4 + 4 = 8 legs on a spider.

5 + 5 = 10 fingers.

6 + 6 = 12, a dozen.

7 + 7 = 14, a common football score of two touchdowns.

8 + 8 = 16: *8* looks like a racetrack, and *16* is the age you can legally drive.

9 + 9 = 18 wheels on a tractor trailer truck.

Using Dice

You can use a set of six (or more) dice to teach number facts. Ask students to roll the dice and group them by dots to add up to ten. Then have students add any dice left over (not included in the groups) at the end. For example, if the dice are rolled as in *Figure 5.24a*, students make two groups of ten. The one remaining die showing five dots is added to the two groups to total *25*, as in *Figure 5.24b*.

Figure 5.24a: With this roll of the dice, students make two groups of 10 and have 5 left over.

Figure 5.24b: Students make two groups of 10 and add the 5 extra dots to make 25.

Vary the number of times students roll the dice, depending on how quickly they learn the number facts that add to ten and how long the exercise sustains their attention. As students gain skill and confidence, add more dice (see *Figures 5.25* and *5.26*). In addition to helping students learn number facts, this exercise helps students develop organizational skills by teaching them to group in tens.

Figure 5.25: Increase the number of dice as students gain skill.

Figure 5.26: As students gain skill using more dice, add even more.

Use the dice to make it fun for students to learn addition facts. Games not only keep students practicing the basic number facts that add to ten, but they also get students practicing more advanced addition operations. The following four dice games students can play individually.

Game 1. The student keeps score by recording the number of dots on each roll to determine the highest roll.

Game 2. The student determines the number of required rolls, such as five, and keeps score of the number of dots in each roll, then totals the scores.

Game 3. The student counts the number of rolls it takes to reach a predetermined total (e.g., *100, 200, 250,* or more).

Game 4. The student records how long it takes to add up the dots on a predetermined number of rolls.

When students have time to play with others, have them play the dice games with the *Using Dice* reproducibles on the CD to record who has the highest roll, who reaches a predetermined total first, and who has the fastest time. Group games provide opportunities to complete calculations. Students who have weak basic skills get to improve them and, as they improve, can be taught how to complete the more advanced calculations for the scoring.

Playing with Large Numbers

Students love to play with large numbers, the larger the better. Students can improve their mental math skills by practicing basic number facts using large numbers. For example, students can practice adding *20* to other numbers:

$20 + 10 = 30$ $20 + 5 = 25$

$20 + 20 = 40$ $20 + 9 = 29$

$20 + 40 = 60$

It may not be evident to students that these calculations are related to the basic number facts that they know (see *Figure 5.27*). Many times students need to have the connection pointed out—usually not once, but often—until the concept is clearly understood. Provide practice with the *Playing with Large Numbers* reproducibles on the CD.

Guides for Counting Fractions

Calculations		Related Number Facts			
$20 + 10 = 30$		$2 + 1 = 3$			
$20 + 20 = 40$		$2 + 2 = 4$			
$20 + 40 = 60$		$2 + 4 = 6$			
$20 + 5 = 25$		$10 + 5 = 15$			
$20 + 9 = 29$		$10 + 9 = 19$			
$100 + 10 = 110$		$10 + 1 = 11$			
$100 + 70 = 70$		$10 + 7 = 17$			
$100 + 100 = 200$		$10 + 10 = 20$		$1 + 1 = 2$	
$100 + 600 = 700$		$10 + 60 = 70$		$1 + 6 = 7$	
$1000 + 500 = 1,500$		$10 + 5 = 15$			
$3000 + 4000 = 7,000$		$3 + 4 = 7$			
$5000 + 300 = 5,300$		$50 + 3 = 53$			

Figure 5.27: Show students the connections between larger-number equations and basic number facts.

Show students that they can do computations with large numbers without writing them on paper. Students with poor math skills usually need to be shown how to add large numbers mentally and that, with practice, they can improve their mental math skills. Having students mentally add *5 billion* and *8 billion* gives them practice in the number fact *5 + 8 = 13*. When students play with numbers, they have a different attitude than when they must work with them.

Adding Columns of Numbers

Adding machines, calculators, and computers have made the task of adding large columns of numbers quick and easy. The following techniques provide both a way to add columns when no machine is handy and a way to compensate for learning difficulties. Students who do not have difficulties with math are able to remember the numbers as they add each number in a column, but many students find it difficult to hold numbers in their heads. They forget the numbers as they add, or they are triggered to another number. For example, when adding: *9 + 8 + 5 + 4*, students might add this way: *9 + 8 = 17 + 5* and then forget that *17* is the number being added to 5, so they must start over. Likewise, students may be triggered in this sequence: *9 + 8 = 17 + 5 = 22;*

23 + 4 = 27. The jump from *22* to *23* is the trigger (see Chapter 2, *Racing Mind* for more about triggers). This explains how students can make errors even though they can add.

This same phenomenon, triggering, creates difficulties when using a calculator. Students read a number and, as they enter it into the calculator, their thoughts trigger to another number, often the next number. For example, when intending to enter *8* into the calculator, students enter *9*. They think *8* and then enter *9*, resulting in an incorrect answer. This can be very frustrating for students when they are adding many numbers.

The following techniques help students add columns and also improve organizational skills. Teach students to preview tasks before they begin work so that they can decide the best way to group numbers. This organizational skill, when combined with other organizational skills, helps students develop the habit of studying how to proceed with a problem rather than impulsively starting or rushing through in an ineffective manner.

Students who make frequent errors need to check their answers. The following techniques enable checking. The problems are laid out in a visual format so that students can go back and check each computation for accuracy. Writing out each computation takes more time than adding straight down a column of numbers, but for students who makes frequent errors, making sure the answers are correct is worth the extra time.

The "Strike Ten" Technique

The "strike ten" technique is an easy way to add a column of numbers between *1* and *9*. It helps students analyze numbers by looking for the patterns in them. *Figure 5.28* demonstrates the steps of the "strike ten" technique:

1. Students strike out any two or more numbers that add to *10*.

2. Each time a number combination adds to *10*, they write *10* next to the column.

3. Students add the tens together, along with any number(s) that remain.

4. Students check their answers by striking out the numbers again, changing the slashes into *X*s.

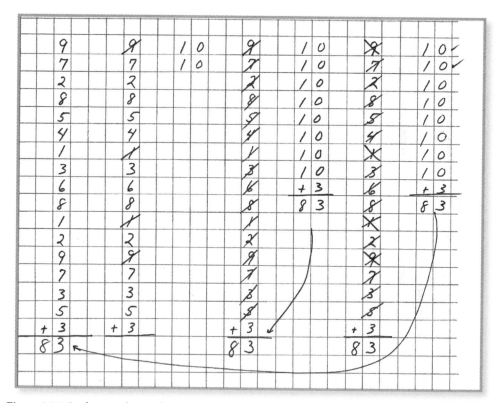

Figure 5.28: Students strike out the numbers that add to ten. In the last column, students check their work.

Some students will automatically begin adding the smallest numbers (ones and twos) together because they seem easier. In *Figure 5.29*, students may combine *1, 2, 3,* and *4* to make *10* rather than *1* and *9, 2* and *8, 3* and *7,* and *4* and *6.* Teach students to start with the larger numbers first. *Figure 5.29* is an excellent set of numbers to use to teach the "strike ten" technique because it has a good mix of digits between *1* and *9.* Provide practice with the *Columns of Numbers: Strike Ten* reproducibles on the CD.

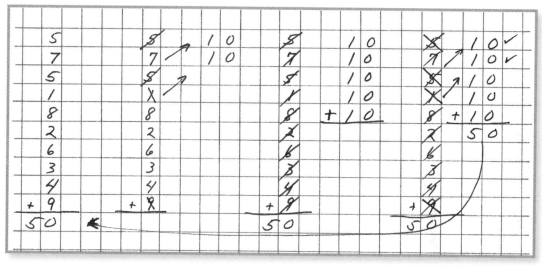

Figure 5.29: Using the "strike ten" technique to add a long column of numbers.

The Pairing Technique

Some columns of numbers do not have a good mix of digits that easily produce combinations of ten. Students can easily add up these columns of numbers by pairing. Adding columns this way also makes the computations easy to check. This technique makes all of the calculations visible so that students can check each one quickly and easily.

Figure 5.30 shows the steps for adding a column of numbers using pairing. Students pair off all the numbers in the column and add up the two numbers in each pair. Then they pair the numbers again and add them together. Students proceed with pairing and adding pairs until they have one final number (the answer). Students then check their addition of each pair, circling the pairs as they go (see *Figure 5.31*).

The pairing technique works well with all columns of numbers, even those that have a good number mix for the "strike ten" technique (as demonstrated in *Figure 5.32*). Provide practice with the *Columns of Numbers: Pairing* reproducibles on the CD.

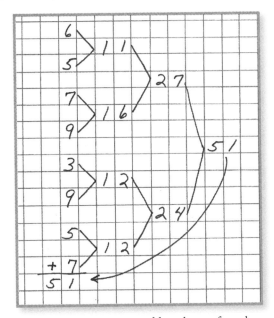

Figure 5.30: Using pairing to add a column of numbers.

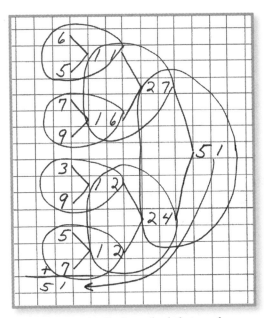

Figure 5.31: Students check their work.

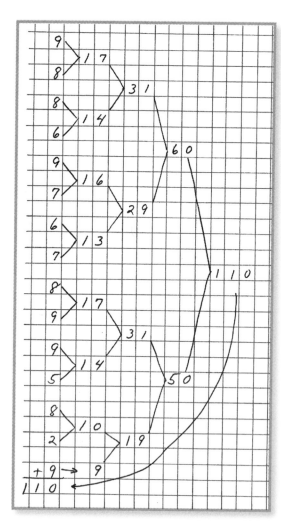

Figure 5.32: The pairing technique applied to a column of numbers that could also be solved using the "strike ten" technique.

The Multiplying Technique

Students who know the multiplication facts can use multiplication to add columns of numbers. *Figure 5.33* illustrates the steps:

1. Students count the number of times each digit appears in the column; for example, 5 appears three times.

2. They write the digit and the number of times it appears beside the column; for example 5 x 3.

3. Students multiply each digit by the number of times it appears to obtain a product for each one (e.g., 5 x 3 = 15).

4. Students add up the products, using the pairing method or adding the products together one by one. (*Figure 5.33* shows both methods.)

5. Students check their computations.

Provide practice with the *Columns of Numbers: Multiplying* reproducibles on the CD.

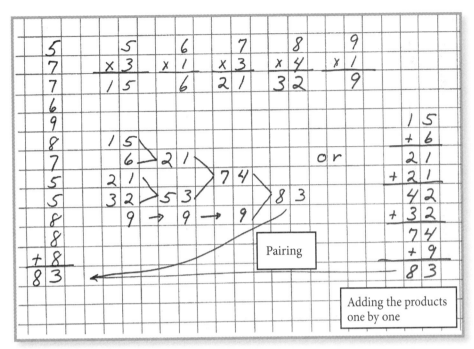

Figure 5.33: Using the multiplying technique to add a column of numbers.

Mixed Techniques

When students become proficient with the three techniques for adding columns, show them how to combine them. They may use two or all three of the techniques. In *Figure 5.34*, students strike out pairs that add to ten ("strike ten"), pair some of the numbers (pairing), and multiply some of the digits (multiplying).

Be sure that students with poor organizational skills keep the mixture of techniques well organized so that they do not become confused or miss some of the numbers. Suggest that students use a different color for each technique to help them stay organized and facilitate the checking of their work (as in *Figure 5.35*). Provide practice with the *Columns of Numbers: Mixed Techniques* reproducible on the CD.

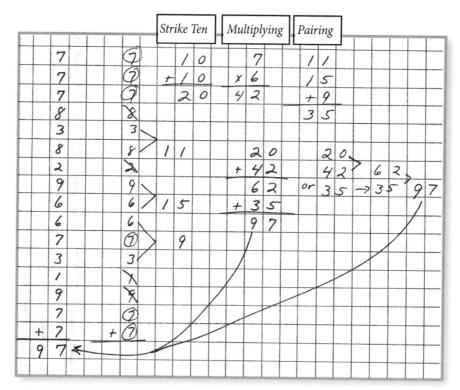

Figure 5.34: An example of using mixed techniques to add a long column of numbers.

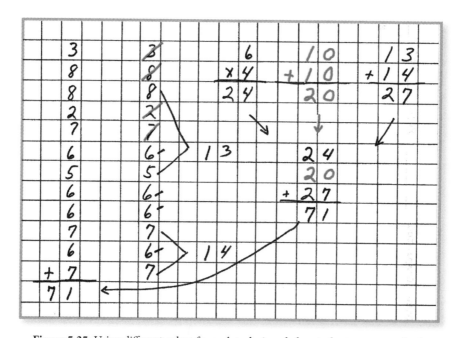

Figure 5.35: Using different colors for each technique helps students stay organized

Breaking Apart Multidigit Numbers

Students who have difficulty with large numbers can learn to break them into manageable chunks using this technique. Although this technique takes time, it does have advantages. First of all, it makes the calculations clearly visible. Second, it reduces or eliminates carrying. And third, it facilitates the checking of computations. This technique also helps students who have problems carrying or holding numbers in their minds.

Figure 5.36 shows how to rewrite a column of multidigit numbers by adding zeros:

1. Students write out each number by adding zeros, beginning with the largest place value, in this case, the ten-thousand place (*50,000* and *30,000*).

2. Students proceed to write out each number from highest to lowest, adding zeros, until all the numbers are listed (see the second column in *Figure 5.36*).

3. Students then pair the numbers and combine them (as in the pairing technique). For example, *50,000* and *30,000* are paired and added together to produce *80,000*.

4. Students write the products of the pairs in a column and add them together to determine the sum (see the third column in *Figure 5.36*).

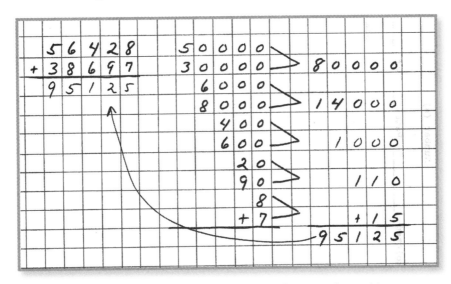

Figure 5.36: Students rewrite multidigit numbers with zeros and use pairing to determine the sum.

This technique can also be used to add columns of double-digit numbers, as in *Figure 5.37*. Instruct students with weak mental math skills to write out each number. For students who have difficulty understanding place value, add a counting step: Instruct them to count the places to the right of the digit in the equation, write that number of zeros in a new column, and then write in the digit at the beginning of the zeros.

As students develop their skills, they may combine numbers before they write them down. For example in *Figure 5.38*, *300* and *400* are paired and combined for *700*, but the student only writes *700*. *100* and *500* are paired and combined for *600*. *20* and *80* are paired and combined for *100*, as is the *60* and *40*. *8* and *2* are paired and combined for *10*. *9* and *7* are paired and combined for *16*. Each set is added, and the sums are added together for the final answer.

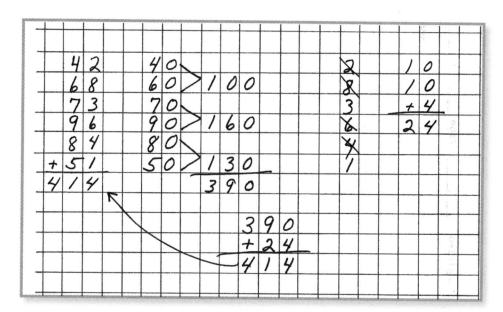

Figure 5.37: Rewriting double-digit equations by adding zeros eliminates carrying.

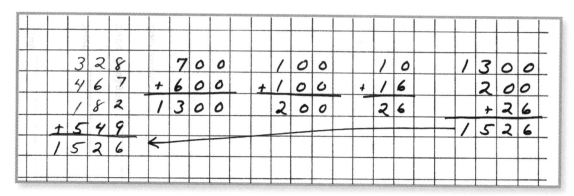

Figure 5.38: As students advance, they can combine pairs without writing them down.

Figure 5.39 illustrates how to rewrite a large multidigit equation by adding zeros and then combining the pairs to obtain the total. The time lost by rewriting the numbers is offset by the elimination of carrying and the ease of checking each computation.

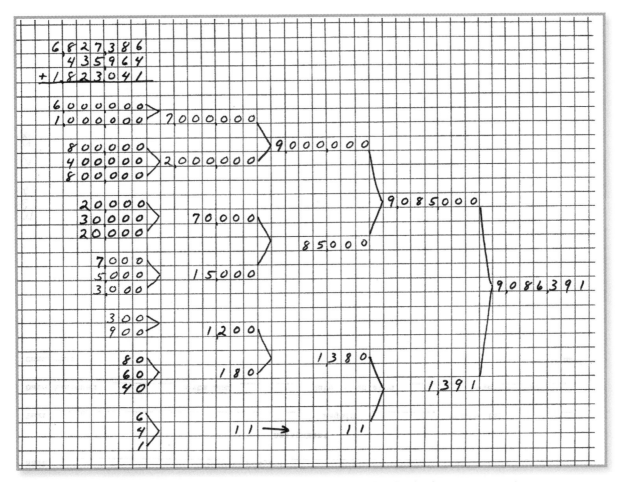

Figure 5.39: Breaking a multidigit equation into manageable chunks eliminates carrying and makes the computations easy to check.

Addressing Problems With Carrying

Many students with moderate-to-severe learning problems have difficulty with the concept of carrying. Use the following techniques and the *Carrying Digits* reproducibles on the CD to help students master carrying.

Carrying to Friendly Numbers

This technique involves carrying to a "friendly" number rather than to the top of the next column. A **friendly number** is one that will combine to make ten or that the student can easily add. *Figure 5.40* shows the typical way students are taught to carry numbers when adding. *Figure 5.41* demonstrates how carrying to friendly numbers makes addition easier. For example, in the first problem the *2* that is carried from adding the right-hand digits is given to the *8* in the left-hand column to make *10*. Then students add the other two numbers to the *10*.

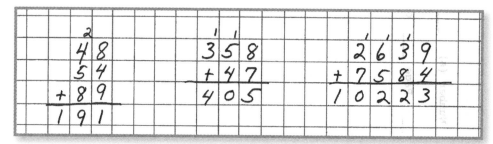

Figure 5.40: The typical way to solve addition problems by carrying to the top of the next column.

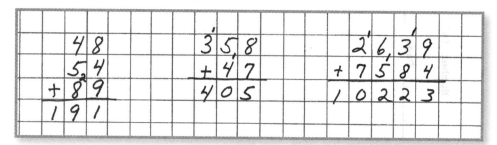

Figure 5.41: Solving addition problems by carrying to friendly numbers that combine to make 10 or to make other easily combined numbers, such as 5.

Mnemonic Clues for Carrying

Students who have right/left discrimination problems often have difficulty remembering which number to carry when they are adding. Use mnemonic clues to help them remember which number to carry. The following four clues help students with the operation of carrying.

1. **The right side.** *Figure 5.42* shows a common error in carrying. When adding *9* and *6* to make *15*, students may write down 1 and carry the *5* instead of the other way around. Slowing down the process and teaching students to associate the right side of their bodies with the number that is written under the line helps to prevent this error. You can also teach students to associate the number to be carried with the left side of the bodies.

    In addition, provide a saying or other memory clue that reminds students to focus on the operation of carrying so that they don't just automatically write the numbers. It's the automatic response that often causes the error. For example, instruct students to tap their pencils twice in the spot where they are going to write the number and to say the number before writing it.

2. **Heavy numbers.** This technique involves teaching students to "feel" the heaviness of the number to be written below the line and the lightness of the number to be carried. In *Figure 5.43*, students add *8* and *4* to get *12*. The *2* is the "heavier" digit, the *1* is smaller (and so can be perceived as the "lighter" of the two digits). The *2* is heavier, so it stays under the line. Students then know to carry the *1*.

    If the number is *0*, as in the second example in *Figure 5.43*, have students associate *0* with a rock and "feel" its heaviness. This technique is an effective memory tool for many students.

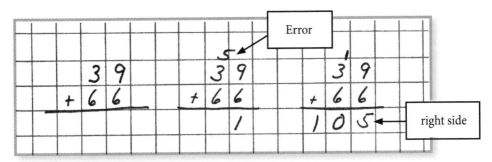

Figure 5.42: A common error is to carry the wrong digit.

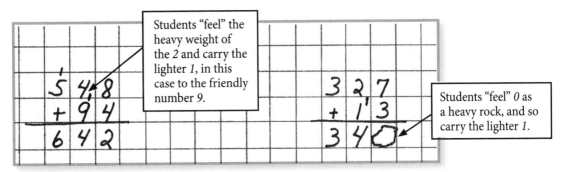

Figure 5.43: Carrying the "lighter" numbers and keeping the "heavy" numbers below the line.

3. **Carrying 10.** In this technique, students learn to carry *10*. This prevents the error of carrying the wrong number, as in *Figure 5.44* where the *4* is incorrectly carried instead of the *1*. Teach students to carry the number *10*, writing the number above the equation as shown in the figure. Writing the *0* of the *10* helps students understand the concept of carrying, assists with correct placement, and does not affect the computation.

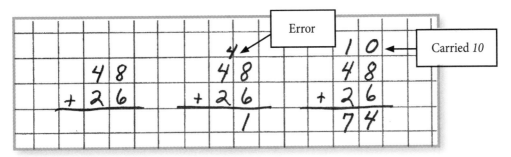

Figure 5.44: Carrying *10* instead of *1* helps students understand carrying and ensures that the correct number is carried.

4. Extra lines. In this technique, students leave a line of space in which they write the numbers carried, as in *Figure 5.45*. The carried numbers are then near the numbers not carried so that students see and can check that the numbers they write are what they want to write. In the figure, the carried *1* and the *4* are near to each other, so students can see that they correctly carried the digits: *14*. Likewise, the *16* and *18* are recognizable even though the two digits in each number are written on different lines.

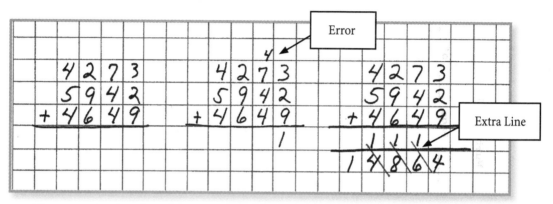

Figure 5.45: Leaving a line of space in which to carry numbers enables students to check that the digits they carry are correct.

Teaching Subtraction

$\dfrac{7}{-4}$ *Students who have difficulty with addition have even more difficulty with subtraction. Students who know only a few subtraction facts by automatic recall must count to calculate most of the number facts when subtracting. Some students who count still come up with the wrong answer because of various processing problems. The following techniques help students complete subtraction successfully. As with the other number facts, automatic recall is the goal, but increased proficiency at any higher level is preferable to counting or guessing.*

Reverse Addition

Show students that subtraction is the reverse of addition. This simple concept is not obvious to all, so don't assume that students automatically see the relationship between addition and subtraction. Use the examples in *Figure 6.1* and the *Reverse Addition* reproducibles on the CD to show this relationship.

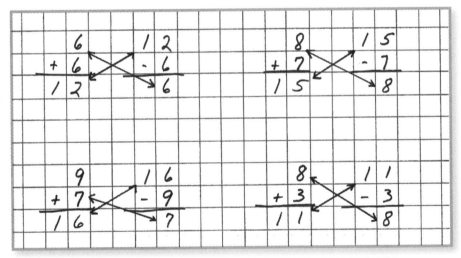

Figure 6.1: Illustrate for students that subtraction is the reverse of addition.

Students who know the multiplication facts by automatic recall, but count or guess addition and subtraction facts, are usually able to master the addition facts and use reverse addition for subtraction. Students who know the multiplication facts can usually learn the addition facts in a few days or in a couple of weeks. Because habits are difficult to break, students may need assistance remembering to use reverse addition when subtracting. Remind them repeatedly to not count or guess when subtracting.

Reverse addition works for students who can learn the addition facts; however, some students cannot learn addition facts because of learning problems. If students do not know the multiplication facts, they may not be able to learn the addition facts quickly, if at all. Reverse addition will not work for these students.

Subtraction Patterns

Seeing the patterns in the number facts helps students understand the concept of subtraction. Then they remember the facts more easily. Share the following five patterns with students, showing them the *Number-Fact Patterns* reproducible (*Figure 6.2*).

Pattern 1: Demonstrate that all the subtraction facts can be seen as addition by reading up instead of down, as in:

$$
\begin{array}{r}
7 \\
-\ 3 \\
\hline
4 \uparrow
\end{array}
$$

Pattern 2: Point out that the totals in each row, going from left to right, increase by one.

Pattern 3: Note that the totals in every line are sequential from *1* to *9*.

Pattern 4: All the answers in a column are the same.

Pattern 5: Have students look at the diagonal from top left to bottom right. The numbers are sequential from *1* to *9*.

Pattern 6: Have students look at the diagonal from top right to bottom left. The numbers are sequential from *9* to *1*.

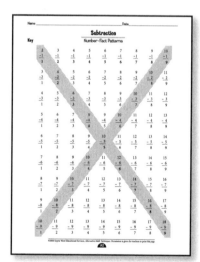

Figure 6.2: The Subtraction: Number-Fact Patterns reproducible shows six subtraction patterns.

Subtracting by Adding

This technique uses the sequence-to-the-right-and-back pattern (introduced in Chapter 5, *Number Patterns*) to help students who have not mastered addition facts to subtract by adding. To subtract a single digit from a teen, such as *14 – 7* in *Figure 6.3*, students take the following steps.

1. If necessary, students write out the sequence-to-the-right-and-back pattern for *10*:

$$\begin{array}{r} 12345 \\ + \ 98765 \\ \hline 10 \end{array}$$

2. Students look at the lower, or bottom, number of the equation (*7*) and determine the number that when added to it would equal *10* (in this case, *3*).

3. Students then write this number (*+ 3*) next to the equation's lower number (so that it reads *7 + 3 = 10*).

4. Students add the number (*3*) diagonally to the digit in the ones column of the larger, or top, number in the equation (*4*) to obtain the total (*4 + 3 = 7*, so the answer to *14 –7 is 7*).

The same technique is used in *Figure 6.3* with the other three equations. Use the *Subtracting by Adding* reproducibles on the CD to provide practice.

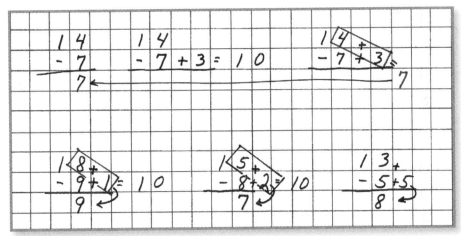

Figure 6.3: To subtract from a teen, students determine the number that when added to the bottom number will equal 10, then add that number to the digit in the ones place of the top number.

Subtracting From the Borrowed 10

Some students, especially those who have difficulty with visual processing, find borrowing difficult. This technique allows students to see the numbers and keep track of their steps. It also reduces the number of the subtraction facts that the students need to know. Use it as a transitional technique while students are working on mastering the number facts by automatic recall.

In *Figure 6.4*, students take the following steps to solve *42 – 18 =*:

1. Students borrow *10* from the *4* in the tens place, the *40*, crossing out the *4* and making it *3*. They write *10* above the *2* in the ones place.

2. Next, they subtract *8* from the *10* and write the result, *2*, below the line.

3. Students take the number from the top line of the equation (in this case, *2*) and write it below the result (in this case, also *2*).

4. They add these together to get *4*.

5. Students complete the problem by subtracting *1* from the *3* to get the total, *24*.

Provide practice with *The Borrowed 10* reproducible on the CD.

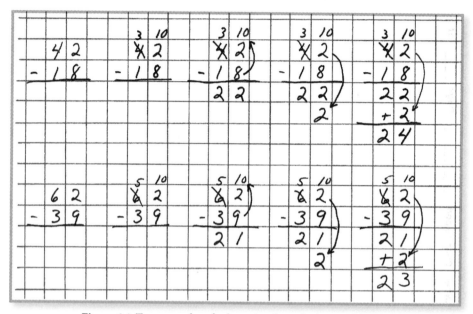

Figure 6.4: Two examples of subtracting from the borrowed 10.

Eliminating Borrowing

Students use this technique to change numbers so that there is no need to borrow. It is not a common technique, but it is worth demonstrating to students because it helps them understand how numbers relate.

In *Figure 6.5*, students evaluate the problem, *82 – 67 =*, noting that *2* is less than *7* and therefore needs to be changed. Students add *3* to the *67*, rewriting it as *70*. Then they add *3* to the *82*, rewriting it as *85*. *85 – 70 = 15*, so *82 – 67 = 15*. As long as students add the same amount to both numbers, the answer will be correct. The same technique is used in the other two examples in the figure.

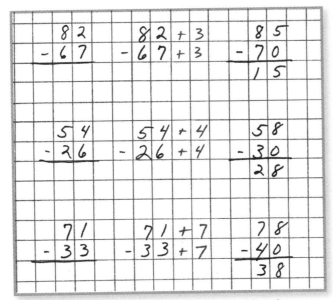

Figure 6.5: Students eliminate borrowing by adding the same amount to each number in the equation.

In *Figure 6.6*, the two problems are rewritten twice. First the tens column is changed, then the hundreds column is changed. *Figure 6.7* shows a problem rewritten three times. Although rewriting takes time, many students find it less confusing than borrowing. Consequently they take less time rewriting than they do when borrowing. This technique also introduces students to the concept that "what you do to one side of an equation, you do to the other." Use the *Eliminating Borrowing* reproducibles on the CD to provide practice.

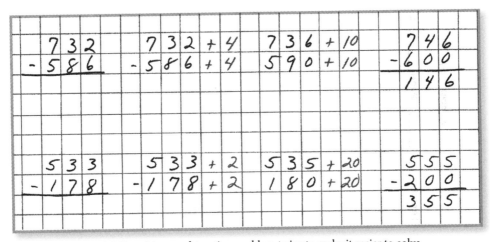

Figure 6.6: Rewriting a subtraction problem twice to make it easier to solve.

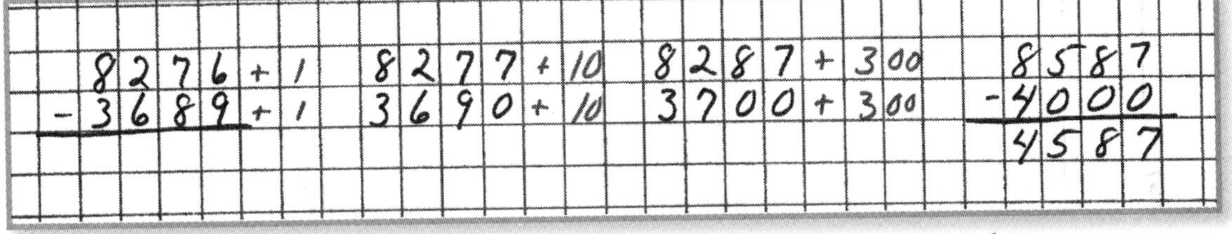

Figure 6.7: Rewriting a subtraction problem three times to make it easier to solve.

Subtracting Without Borrowing

This technique works well for students who find borrowing confusing but are able to use patterns in numbers to complete computations. This technique is easiest to use with small numbers (less than *1,000*). However, as students become proficient with the technique, they will be able to use it with large numbers as well. As students use it, they also find other number combinations easier to work with. Students who have not yet mastered addition facts may need to write out the sequence-to-the-right-and-back pattern for *10* (see Chapter 5, *Number Patterns*) before using this technique.

Students visualize a number line and choose the number with the most zeros that lies between the two numbers of the equation. In *Figure 6.8*, 100 lies between *103* and *97* on the number line. Students see that *103* is three numbers away from 100 and that 97 is three numbers away from *100*. Students add the number differences to answer the equation (*3 + 3 = 6, so 103 – 97 = 6*). The second example in *Figure 6.8* is similar to the first.

The examples in *Figure 6.9* demonstrate how students use the technique with larger numbers. In the first example in the figure, students write *100* between *112* and *88*, and see that *112* is *12* more than *100*. They may not see that *88* is *12* less than *100*, but, by writing *90* (the number with the most zeros between *100* and *88*), the *10* and *2* become obvious. Students then add up all the number differences (*12, 10,* and *2*) to solve the equation: *24*.

In the second example in *Figure 6.9*, students write the numbers *200, 100,* and *70* between *225* and *69*. They write *25* (*225 – 200*), 100 (*200 – 100*), 30 (*100 – 70*) and 1 (*70 – 69*) and then add these numbers to get *156*, the result of *225 – 69*. Provide practice with the *Subtracting Without Borrowing* reproducibles on the CD.

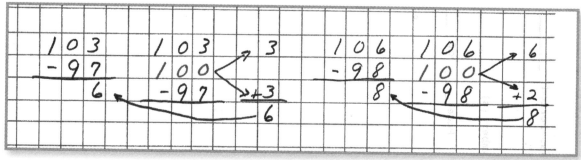

Figure 6.8: Students subtract without borrowing by adding up the differences between numbers.

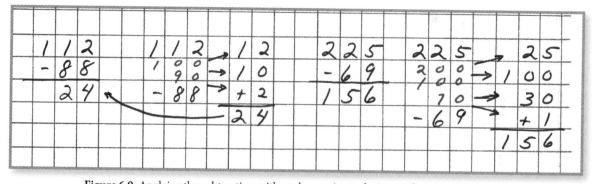

Figure 6.9: Applying the subtracting-without-borrowing technique to larger numbers.

Breaking Apart Multidigit Numbers

Teach students to break apart large numbers into manageable chunks to subtract them, using a similar technique to the one presented in Chapter 5, *Breaking Apart Multidigit Numbers*. When subtracting numbers that do not require borrowing, students rewrite the numbers by adding zeros. To subtract numbers that require borrowing, students use a mixture of techniques.

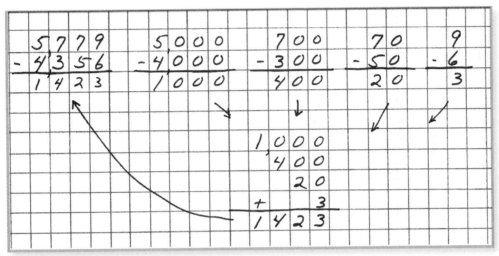

Figure 6.10: Students rewrite multidigit numbers with zeros, subtract them, and add the differences together to determine the sum.

In *Figure 6.10*, students first rewrite the numbers in thousands, hundreds, and tens by adding zeros. Second, they do the subtraction. And, finally, they add the differences to determine the answer. Use the *Subtraction: Breaking Apart Multidigit Numbers* reproducibles on the CD to provide practice.

In *Figure 6.11*, students are presented with a subtraction problem that requires borrowing. To solve it, they combine this technique with the technique for eliminating borrowing (see *Eliminating Borrowing* earlier in this chapter). First, students rewrite the thousands by adding zeros and subtract. Second, they add *1* to the hundreds in order to eliminate borrowing and subtract. Then they add the two sums to determine the answer.

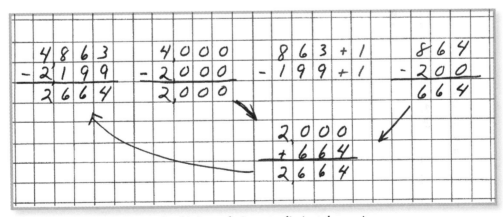

Figure 6.11: Combining techniques to eliminate borrowing.

When combining techniques, students need to keep the operations organized so that they do not become confused. The example in *Figure 6.12* shows how students can use a different color for each operation to aid in organization.

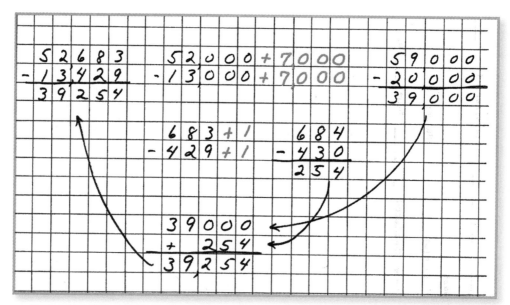

Figure 6.12: Using different colors helps students stay organized when combining techniques.

Chapter 7

Teaching Multiplication

9
×1

The number facts of multiplication are more difficult than addition and subtraction for some students because the patterns are less obvious and the products are larger numbers. Many students are in the habit of counting or calculating the multiplication facts, and these habits do not result in automatic recall of the facts. Counting is very time consuming, so students who count commonly respond to multiplication by guessing or avoiding it.

Encourage students to learn the multiplication facts by automatic recall, but keep in mind that some learning problems make this task difficult, if not impossible. The primary learning problem that affects multiplication is either/or confusion caused by right/left discrimination problems (also see Chapter 2, Right/Left Discrimination). Students confuse similar facts and have both the correct and incorrect answers in their memories.

The second learning problem that affects multiplication is the racing mind (also see Chapter 2, Racing Mind). Students with racing minds may be triggered, thinking one number and saying or writing another.

Students who count or calculate the multiplication facts never really learn them. They are frequently frustrated because it takes too long to complete multiple-step problems. If a student has not been able to learn the times tables during the third grade, and still doesn't know them in fifth grade, then the alternative methods in this chapter should be tried. These methods will help you teach students the times tables and how to solve multiplication problems.

Multiplication as Shortcut

Show students that multiplication is a shortcut of addition and that addition is a shortcut of counting. This helps students understand why counting or calculating the multiplication facts makes completing math problems difficult. Have students play the Shortcut Game in small groups or time themselves when playing the game as a solo activity.

The Shortcut Game. Divide students into three groups. One group multiplies, the second group adds, and the third group counts to find the answers to the six problems in *Figure 7.1* and the *Shortcut Game* reproducibles. Each group records the time it takes to find the answer to each problem. Post the times so that students understand the value of learning higher-level skills.

Comparing Multiplication, Adding, and Counting

No.	Multiply	Add	Count	Ans.
1.	2 × 2 =	2 + 2 =	1 1 1 1	4
2.	6 × 2 =	2 + 2 + 2 + 2 + 2 + 2 =	1 1 1 1 1 1 1 1 1 1 1 1	12
3.	6 × 7 =	6 + 6 + 6 + 6 + 6 + 6 + 6 =	1 1 1 1 1 1 1 1 1 1 1 1 1 1 1 1 1 1 1 1 1 1 1 1 1 1 1 1 1 1 1 1 1 1 1 1 1 1 1 1 1 1 1 1 1 1 1 1	42
4.	9 × 9 =	9 + 9 + 9 + 9 + 9 + 9 + 9 + 9 + 9 =	1 1 1 1 1 1 1 1 1 1 1 1 1 1 1 1 1 1 1 1 1 1 1 1 1 1 1 1 1 1 1 1 1 1 1 1 1 1 1 1 1 1 1 1 1 1 1 1 1 1 1 1 1 1 1 1 1 1 1 1 1 1 1 1 1 1 1 1 1 1 1 1 1 1 1 1 1 1 1 1 1 1 1 1 1 1 1	81
5.	12 × 11 =	12 + 12 + 12 + 12 + 12 + 12 + 12 + 12 + 12 + 12 + 12 =	1 1	132
6.	23 × 14 =	23 + 23 + 23 + 23 + 23 + 23 + 23 + 23 + 23 + 23 + 23 + 23 + 23 + 23 =	1 1	322

Figure 7.1:

Mnemonic Clues for Multiplying

Develop mnemonic clues for the multiplication facts that students find difficult to remember. Not every number fact requires a mnemonic clue; some are more difficult to remember than others. Following are a few mnemonics for multiplication facts. With a little encouragement and their own creativity, students can also develop their own mnemonic clues.

Three sixes. The multiplication fact $6 \times 6 = 36$ has three sixes.

Sequence. For $8 \times 7 = 56$ and $7 \times 8 = 56$, remember the sequence *5678*.

Touchdowns. Associate $7 \times 7 = 49$ with football: 6 points for a touchdown and an extra point for kicking is *7*. Think of two touchdowns (7s) scored by the San Francisco 49ers.

Singing the times tables. Musical melodies and rhythms are effective auditory mnemonic clues for many students, but the number of students who can learn number facts using music is probably smaller than the number who can learn by other methods. The older the students, the less likely they are to try music as a learning tool. Don't expect all students to use music with the same success. Try it, but if it does not make the task of learning the times tables easier, try something else.

Number relationships. Show students how to use number relationships to calculate multiplication facts. One technique is to divide a large number in half, multiply it, and double the product; for example:

8×6 is the same as $4 \times 6 = 24$, doubled to *48*.
8×9 is the same as $4 \times 9 = 36$, doubled to *72*.

Students who use this technique can usually learn the multiplication facts by automatic recall if they practice. Have them list the number facts they are able to successfully use doubling with. Then have students study them until they are mastered.

Number Patterns

Similar to addition- and subtraction-fact patterns, multiplication patterns help some students understand and learn the number facts. Note the three patterns in *Figure 7.2*:

Pattern 1: Point out to students that the products are the same vertically and horizontally for each number.

Pattern 2: Note that many more of the multiplication facts have even products (56) than odd products (25).

Pattern 3: The products of the multiplication facts that begin with odd numbers alternate odd and even.

Use the *Multiplication: Number-Fact Patterns* reproducibles on the CD to provide practice.

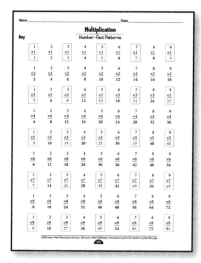

Figure 7.2: The *Multiplication: Number-Fact Patterns* reproducible shows three multiplication-fact patterns.

Patterns of Nine

Show students the products of the nine-times table and demonstrate that when the digits are added together they equal *9*:

$$9 \times 1 = 9 \quad (0 + 9 = 9)$$
$$9 \times 2 = 18 \quad (1 + 8 = 9)$$
$$9 \times 3 = 27 \quad (2 + 7 = 9)$$
$$9 \times 4 = 36 \quad (3 + 6 = 9)$$
$$9 \times 5 = 45 \quad (4 + 5 = 9)$$
$$9 \times 6 = 54 \quad (5 + 4 = 9)$$
$$9 \times 7 = 63 \quad (6 + 3 = 9)$$
$$9 \times 8 = 72 \quad (7 + 2 = 9)$$
$$9 \times 9 = 81 \quad (8 + 1 = 9)$$

Another pattern of the nine-times table students may find useful is to write the numbers *9* to *0* in descending order in a column and then, beginning in front of the *8*, to write the numbers *1* to *9* in ascending order:

9	9
8	18
7	27
6	36
5	45
4	54
3	63
2	72
1	81
0	90

Use the *Patterns of Nine* reproducibles on the CD to provide practice.

Alternating Patterns

One notable pattern in the products of the multiplication facts is that the digits in the ones column are the reverse of each other. For example, *9* is the reverse of *1*, *7* is the reverse of *3*, *8* is the reverse of *2*, and *6* is the reverse of *4*, as illustrated in *Figure 7.3*. Provide practice with the *Alternating Pattern* reproducibles on the CD.

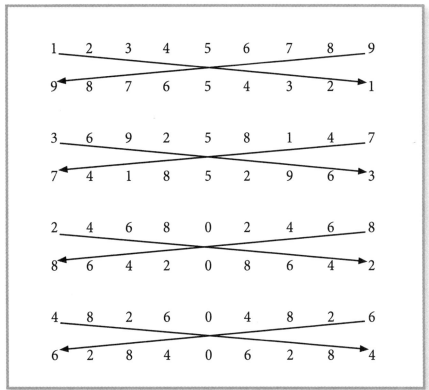

Figure 7.3: The alternating patterns of the times tables.

Odd and Even Patterns

Some students find the odd and even patterns of multiplication especially helpful. (If the first product is even, all the products are even. If the first product is odd, every other product is even.)

Odd and even patterns help students remember the multiplication facts. Point out that when students multiply any number by an even number the product is always even. The product is odd only if both numbers being multiplied are odd. Help students remember these patterns using the visual in *Figure 7.4*.

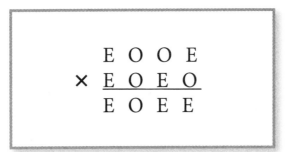

Figure 7.4: Visual clue for multiplication.

When students understand the patterns, show them how they can use them to do quick checks of their answers, as in *Figure 7.5*. Provide practice with the *Multiplication: Odd and Even Patterns* reproducibles on the CD.

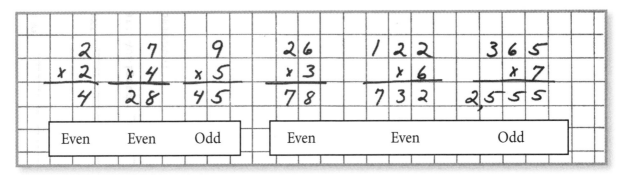

Figure 7.5: Students check their multiplication answers using the odd and even patterns.

Counting

Motivate students with counting exercises that show they can do things they thought were beyond their ability.

Sequence Exercises

The rhythm of the number sequences in *Figure 7.6* helps students learn the multiplication facts. Students use the sequences in a repeating pattern to count by twos, fours, sixes, and eights. Have students practice counting beyond ten times the first number of the sequence (i.e., beyond *20, 40, 60,* or *80*) so that they gain confidence and become familiar with the sets of numbers that make up the multiplication facts.

It is recommended that students complete the exercises both orally and in writing. Oral exercises help develop the rhythm of the sequence of numbers. Written exercises help students see the repeating patterns.

Instruct students to use the five-number sequence in large print as a guide to counting by intervals. For example, students use the first sequence in *Figure 7.6* to count by twos. They count *2, 4, 6, 8*, and change the *0* to *10*. Then they go back to the beginning of the sequence, counting *12, 14, 16, 18*, and *20*. Using the sequence, students can continue counting as long as they want to.

2 4 6 8 0

2	4	6	8	10	12	14	16	18	20	22	24	26
28	30	32	34	36	38	40	42	44	46	48	50	52

4 8 2 6 0

4	8	12	16	20	24	28	32	36	40	44	48	52
56	60	64	68	72	76	80	84	88	92	96	100	104

6 2 8 4 0

6	12	18	24	30	36	42	48	54	60	66	72	78
84	90	96	102	108	114	120	126	132	138	144	150	156

8 6 4 2 0

8	16	24	32	40	48	56	64	72	80	88	96	104
112	120	128	136	144	152	160	168	176	184	192	200	208

Figure 7.6: Students use the *Multiplication: Counting by Even Intervals* reproducibles to practice counting by intervals.

Through practice, students learn the patterns well enough that they can count by intervals without using the five-number sequence as a reference. Students may also use the sequences to count in higher intervals; for example *24680* becomes *12, 24, 36, 48, 60*, and so on. Using the sequence *48260*, students can count by fourteens: *14, 28, 42, 56, 70, 84*, and so on.

Multiplication Success

I teach the counting exercises to all my students who struggle with the multiplication facts. Tom was one such student who gained confidence using these exercises. With practice and the help of a few mnemonic clues for some odd products, he mastered the multiplication facts. He knew some of the multiplication facts, and by practicing the counting exercises the times tables became familiar.

Counting by Large Intervals

Have students practice reading the numbers in *Figures 7.7* and *7.8* until they become familiar with how numbers work. With enough practice, students will be able to recall these intervals without referring to the lists. Use the *Counting by Large Intervals* reproducibles on the CD to provide extra practice.

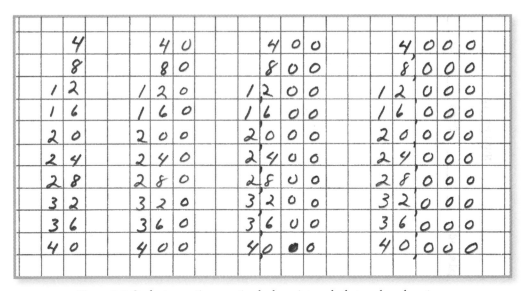

Figure 7.7: Students practice counting by large intervals that are based on 4.

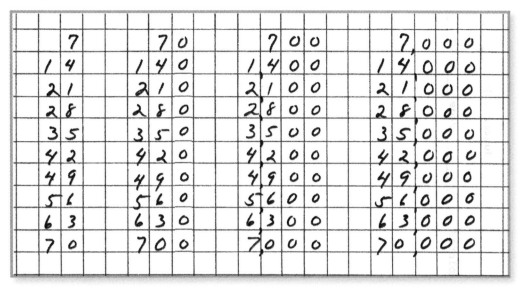

Figure 7.8: Students practice counting by large intervals that are based on 7.

Multiple-Step Operations

Some students have difficulty understanding and remembering the procedures for multiple-digit multiplication. They forget how to use zeros as placeholders or they skip steps (e.g., failing to multiply all the numbers in a problem). One way to help them eliminate these errors is to add a few extra steps that serve as reminders.

Mark the steps. Students begin by drawing a box around the digit they are multiplying. When they have finished multiplying this boxed digit, they draw an *X* through the box as a reminder that they have finished with this digit (see *Figure 7.9*). Drawing an *X* through the box reminds them to place a *0* as a placeholder on the next line of the problem. In order to eliminate confusion about which digits they have carried, students circle the carried digits. Once circled, students can ignore them. The process is repeated until all the digits are multiplied as illustrated in *Figure 7.9*.

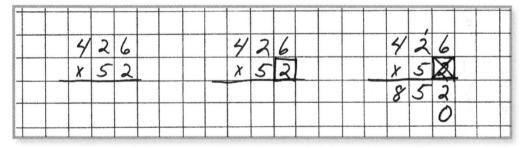

Figure 7.9: Students draw a square around a number in a multiple-step problem.

Figure 7.10 demonstrates how taking a few extra steps ensures that students accurately complete the operations. Provide practice with the *Multiple-Step Operations* reproducibles on the CD.

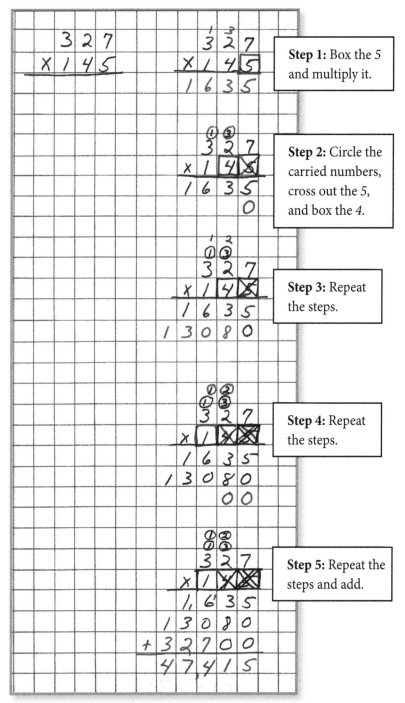

Figure 7.10: Students draw boxes and cross out digits to help them keep track of the operations.

Breaking Apart Multidigit Numbers

One way to help students multiply numbers with two or more digits is to demonstrate that the numbers can be broken apart and calculated separately, as in *Figures 7.11* and *7.12*. This technique is most helpful for students who have difficulty completing all the steps in a multiple-step process. Use the *Multiplication: Breaking Apart Multidigit Numbers* reproducibles on the CD to provide practice.

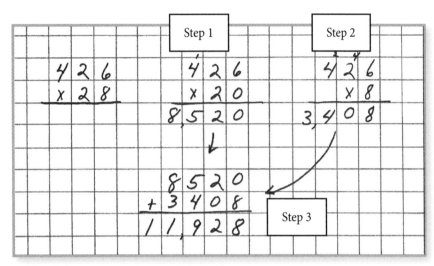

Figure 7.11: Students break multidigit problems into manageable chunks and then add the products to get the answer.

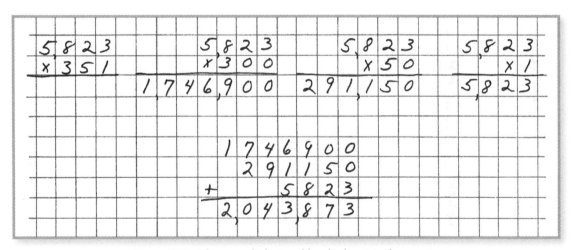

Figure 7.12: A larger multidigit problem broken into three parts.

Teaching Division

Many students appear to not understand the concept of division when completing math activities; however, they are quite capable of using division in real life. Students with poor math skills usually have no difficulty dividing a candy bar in half to share with a friend or dividing food into four platefuls. Students who play musical instruments understand that there are four beats in a measure and have no problem equating an eighth note with half of a beat.

Yet, students who have underdeveloped math skills are usually unable to complete calculations of division even though they understand the concept. They may know how to divide a cookie in half or a candy bar into three parts, but they usually are not able to complete the same calculations when presented with 1 ÷ 3 = or 1/3. The simple concept of dividing something into parts is disconnected from division computations using numbers and notation.

To add to their confusion, the operation of division is completed in the opposite from that of addition, subtraction, and multiplication when these problems are written vertically (as in Figure 8.1). Those operations are completed from the right to left, but division is done from the left to right. This can be especially confusing for students who have right/left discrimination problems.

$$\begin{array}{ccc} 426 & 587 & 3236 \\ +\ \ 8 & -\ 66 & \times\ 24 \end{array}$$

⟵

Figure 8.1: The operation of division is performed from left to right, whereas the operations of addition, subtraction, and multiplication are performed right to left.

Although for most students this confusion fades over time, some students benefit from the visual clue in *Figure 8.2* that indicates the direction of division.

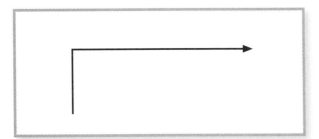

Figure 8.2: This visual clue helps students remember the direction of division operations.

Since the division facts are the reverse of the multiplication facts, students who do not know the multiplication facts are not able to complete division computations without lengthy compensatory techniques or the use of a calculator. Students who use counting to do multiplication usually are not able to reverse the procedure. Furthermore, if students cannot estimate, they cannot do long division without a calculator—and even with a calculator, they often do not know if the answer is correct.

The concept of a **remainder** is difficult for some students to comprehend. You can concretely illustrate this concept using familiar examples, such as dividing a pizza into fourths for three students: Each student gets a piece and one is left over. But many students do not see the connection between the illustrative examples and the remainders of division problems.

Students are also confused by the symbols used in division. In fact, students with right/left discrimination problems often cannot remember how to set up division problems. They need to be shown the relationship between addition and subtraction facts and between multiplication and division facts. You can use the examples in *Figure 8.3* to create a bookmark or classroom poster that helps students remember the symbols and set-up.

$5 \times 5 = 25$	$25 \div 5 = 5$	$25/5 = 5$	$5 \overline{)\ 25}$ with 5 on top	25 divided by 5 = 5
$6 \times 8 = 48$	$48 \div 6 = 8$	$48/6 = 8$	$6 \overline{)\ 48}$ with 8 on top	48 divided by 6 = 8
$8 \times 6 = 48$	$48 \div 8 = 6$	$48/8 = 6$	$8 \overline{)\ 48}$ with 6 on top	48 divided by 8 = 6

Figure 8.3: Give students reminders of division symbols and problem set-up.

Another common problem students have is not remembering the correct sequence of the operation. Students who find division time consuming and frustrating try to avoid it or rush through the steps to finish the problems as quickly as possible. You can assist students to remember the sequence of the steps of long division using the following techniques.

Talking through the steps. Because long division requires a number of steps, students need to practice the sequence. Have them talk through the operation of long division without doing the calculations. For example, a student talking through the steps of the problem in *Figure 8.4*, says, "I find the number in the four times table that is closest to *31* without going higher than *31*. I place that number on top of the bracket above the *1*. Then I multiply that number by 4 and write the product under the *31*. I subtract that number from the *31* and then write that number underneath. Next I bring the *5* down and write it beside the number. Then I repeat the process."

$$4 \overline{)315}$$

Figure 8.4: Students recite the steps of solving this problem without actually doing the calculations.

Mnemonic clues for dividing. Visual or auditory mnemonic clues help students remember the sequence of operations. Use the visual pattern in *Figure 8.5* to help students remember the step sequence. Or try the auditory mnemonic clues of *E, M, S, Bd, R* (**e**stimate, **m**ultiply, **s**ubtract, **b**ring **d**own, **r**epeat) or *Dad, Mom, Sister, Brother* (**d**ivide, **m**ultiply, **s**ubtract, and **b**ring down).

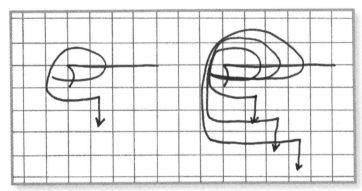

Figure 8.5: Visual mnemonic clues, like this one, help students remember the sequence of steps.

Color coding. Color coding the steps of long division helps students remember the steps and facilitates the checking of their work. Students choose whatever colors they like, but always use the same color for each operation so that they do not become confused.

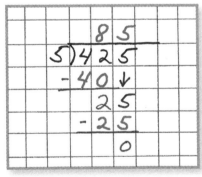

Figure 8.6: Color coding long-division operations.

Customized exercises. Many math exercises progress too quickly to more difficult problems for students with learning problems. Customize your math exercises in order to help students master the procedures and the sequences of operations. Include more simple problems and review the operations before each exercise.

Teaching Fractions, Decimals, and Percentages

Students who have weak quantitative concepts usually find fractions, decimals, and percentages especially confusing. They often do not realize that they are dealing with parts; that the numbers represented by fractions, decimals, and percentages can represent the same quantity; and that a whole can be any quantity. Students who do not understand fractions, decimals, and percentages grow up to be adults who do not understand them.

Fractions

Many students do not understand fractions, even students who otherwise do not have difficulty with math. But many students who find fractions difficult do have learning problems. Students from both groups exhibit similar characteristics when learning or working with fractions. They usually understand and use fractions in daily life, saying "Give me half" and protesting if the portions are not equal. They can fill a glass halfway and explain that it needs another half to be full. But, these same students write *1/2 + 1/2 = 2/4*, having no idea what it means or that the answer is incorrect. Another example relates to telling time. Students may be able to tell time and use a clock for planning, but, when asked how many minutes are in a quarter of an hour, they will report that there are *25* minutes in a quarter of an hour (like *25* cents is a quarter of a dollar).

Most students who have problems with fractions also have difficulty with inversions (see Chapter 2, *Right/Left Discrimination*). They got lost one day when a teacher told them that when the number on the bottom of a fraction is larger, the quantity it represents is smaller. Part of the problem students have with fractions is that they learn at a very early age that ascending numbers (*1, 2, 3*, etc.) represent larger and larger quantities. Fractions do not follow this pattern. As the denominators increase, the quantity gets smaller (*1/2, 1/3, 1/4*, etc.). To add to the confusion, when the numerator increases, the quantity increases (*1/8, 3/8, 5/8*, etc.).

And then there are the **reducible fractions** *2/8, 4/8*, and *6/8* that are missing in the sequence of eighths. Instead of following a predictable pattern of increasing numerators (*1/8, 2/8, 3/8, 4/8, 5/8, 6/8, 7/8*), these quantities are written as *1/4, 1/2, and 3/4*.

Students are also confused by *thirds*. They can divide a whole into three parts and put three parts together to make a whole. But when the parts are represented as a decimal, the thirds do not add up to a whole: *0.999* not *1.0*. For some students who think and learn differently, this is so confusing that they become frustrated and "turn off," avoiding all numbers that are written as fractions.

Some students can complete exercises with fraction diagrams and manipulatives, complete homework correctly, and pass the fractions test, but a short time later they cannot complete calculations with fractions or understand how the numbers of fractions work.

Some students are overwhelmed just by the word *fraction*, believing that it only means numbers written with a line between them. They do not understand that mathematically a fraction means part of a whole.

One way to help students understand fractions, and to make the infinite number of fractions seem more manageable, is to explain that because a fraction is a part of a whole, all fractions exist between *0* and *1* (see *Figure 9.1*). Show students that mixed numbers and improper fractions are just whole numbers combined with a fraction.

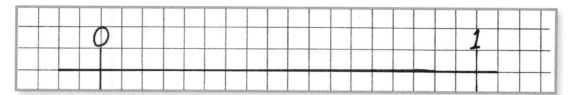

Figure 9.1: Show students that all fractions exist between 0 and 1.

Fractions can be made less intimidating by letting students play with them. Have students write fractions using large numbers such as *1/1000* or *1/22,460* and compare them to *999/1000* or *23,450/23,500*. Show them that the first two fractions are nearly *0* and that the second two are nearly *1* to further help them understand that all fractions exist between *0* and *1*. Take the demonstration a step further by showing students that the fractions *500/1000* and *11,230/22,460* are halfway between *0* and *1*. Depending on age and math level, students may be able to locate other fractions along the continuum.

On a Personal Note:

Students Do the Math but Don't Understand

One adult student explained the confusion she had about numbers, especially fractions, this way: "Numbers were magical, and formulas were potions. The teacher and the other students had this magic and, just like magicians, they could do amusing things that ordinary people could not do."

This is how another one of my students, Jane, felt about fractions. She didn't grasp the concept of fractions as parts of a whole or that wholes could be larger than 1. Jane was good with numbers but just did not relate to them in the real world. She was able to find the answers to problems like 1/4 of 16 by dividing 4 into 16, but was not able to explain what it meant. Like so many students, Jane was confused by the concept but could follow the rules. Following the rules often works for simple calculations, but it is not transferable to higher-level math.

Despite the use of graphics, manipulatives, and language, Jane continued to confuse the concepts of whole, half, double, groups of fours, quarters, and fourths. Other fractions were just as mysterious. Jane was able to complete homework assignments but would randomly fail tests. The repeated use of an exercise that had Jane calculate fractions, decimals, and percentages of various quantities finally resulted in Jane learning to deal with the varying quantities of wholes she found in the real world.

The Pattern of Halves

Half is the easiest fraction to learn and understand. Use the pattern of halves to introduce the concept of dividing numbers into halves. This pattern helps students to understand fractions in general. Ask students to write the numbers *1* to *10* and to write the halves of the even numbers. Then help students see that the halves of the odd numbers are halfway between the halves of the even numbers. When they understand that halves are between the whole numbers, have them write the halves to complete the pattern of halves (see *Figure 9.2*).

Next, teach students that *1/2* can be written as *0.5* and *1 1/2* can be written as *1.5*. Have students practice creating the pattern of halves using both fractions and decimals until they do it with ease. Eventually, many students can mentally recall the pattern of halves.

Step 1: List the numbers *1 to 10*.

Step 2: Write the halves of the even numbers.

Step 3: Write the halves of the odd numbers.

Step 4: Write all the halves as decimals.

Step 1	Step 2	Step 3	Step 4
1	1	1 → ½	1 → .5
2	2 → 1	2 1	2 1
3	3	3 → 1½	3 1.5
4	4 → 2	4 2	4 2
5	5	5 → 2½	5 2.5
6	6 → 3	6 3	6 3
7	7	7 → 3½	7 3.5
8	8 → 4	8 4	8 4
9	9	9 → 4½	9 4.5
10	10 → 5	10 5	10 5

Figure 9.2: Teach students the four steps of the pattern of halves.

When students have mastered the pattern of halves, show them that the pattern also exists in large numbers. Have them play with the pattern, adding more and more zeros to make ever-larger numbers, as in *Figure 9.3*. Students who master the pattern of halves with whole numbers can experiment with decimal numbers, as in *Figure 9.4*. Use the *Fractions, Decimals, and Percentages: Writing the Pattern of Halves* reproducibles on the CD to provide practice.

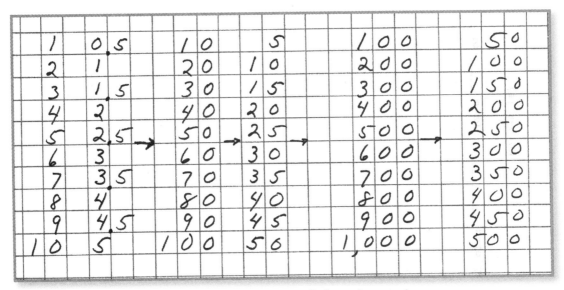

Figure 9.3: Applying the pattern of halves to large numbers.

1	.5	.1	.05	.01	.005	.001	.0005
2	1	.2	.1	.02	.01	.002	.001
3	1.5	.3	.15	.03	.015	.003	.0015
4	2	.4	.2	.04	.02	.004	.002
5	2.5	.5	.25	.05	.025	.005	.0025
6	3	.6	.3	.06	.03	.006	.003
7	3.5	.7	.35	.07	.035	.007	.0035
8	4	.8	.4	.08	.04	.008	.004
9	4.5	.9	.45	.09	.045	.009	.0045
10	5	1.0	.5	.1	.05	.01	.005

Figure 9.4: The pattern of halves used with numbers less than one.

Using the Pattern of Halves

Teach students to use the pattern of halves when reducing fractions (as illustrated in *Figure 9.5*). Have them look for the even numbers in fractions. When students identify even numbers in the numerators and denominators of fractions, they can easily cut each number in half using the pattern of halves.

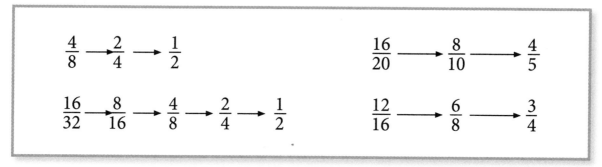

Figure 9.5: Using the pattern of halves to reduce fractions.

Students can use the pattern of halves with whole numbers, too. Show students how to divide whole numbers in half when all the digits are even (see *Figure 9.6*). For whole numbers that contain digits that are odd, have students rewrite the numbers with zeros (see Chapter 5, *Breaking Apart Multidigit Numbers*) and use the pattern of halves to divide them. Then students simply add the numbers together as in *Figure 9.7*. Provide practice with the *Fractions, Decimals, and Percentages: Using the Pattern of Halves* reproducibles on the CD.

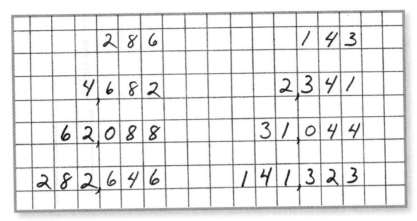

Figure 9.6: Using the pattern of halves to divide even numbers.

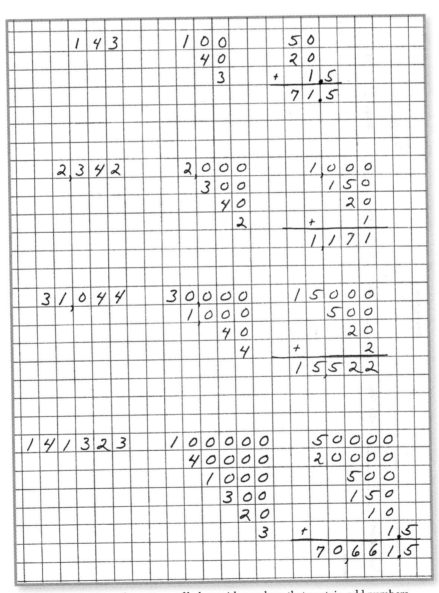

Figure 9.7: Using the pattern of halves with numbers that contain odd numbers.

Corresponding Values

Many students do not realize that fractions, decimals, and percentages are three ways to express the same values. They see these three systems as completely different and distinct. Teach students that each fraction has a decimal and percentage equivalent. Often students better understand fractions when you teach them fractions, decimals, and percentages together. Explain that parts of a whole have different names, depending on whether they are stated as a fraction, decimal, percentage, or term (see *Figure 9.8*). They are mathematical synonyms; the meaning remains the same, like the word *friend* means the same thing in Spanish, French, and German (*amigo, amie,* and *freund*).

Table 9.9 includes **improper fractions** to help students understand how to represent quantities larger than the whole. Some students confuse *doubling* and *dividing*, not knowing which means to *increase* and which means to *decrease*.

Use the *Fractions, Decimals, and Percentages: Corresponding Values* reproducibles on the CD to develop:

- Understanding of how fractional quantities are related to the whole

- Automatic recall of the numbers of fractions, decimals, and percentages.

Figure 9.9 includes *eighths*. Use the reproducible on the CD as a guide to help students add *eighths* to the fractions that they know by automatic recall.

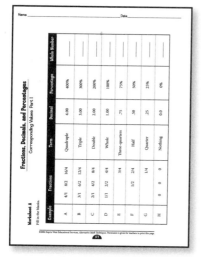

Figure 9.8: The *Fractions, Decimals, and Percentages: Corresponding Values Part I* reproducible gives students practice in fractions, decimals, and percentages.

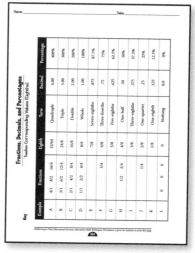

Figure 9.9: The concept of *eighths* is introduced in the *Twelve Corresponding Values* reproducible.

Once students can recall all the fractions, decimals, and percentages in *Figure 9.9*, introduce fifths and tenths using the *Corresponding Values Part II* reproducibles on the CD (*Figure 9.10*). The fractions of *sevenths* and *ninths* are not included in the table because they are not as common, but they can be added later as an advanced exercise.

Figure 9.11 includes *sixteenths*. Point out that there are uncommon fractions missing from the table that can be added.

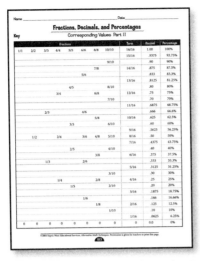

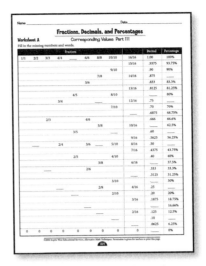

Figure 9.10: Use *The Corresponding Values Part II* reproducibles to introduce *fifths* and *tenths*.

Figure 9.11: *The Corresponding Values Part III* reproducibles introduce *sixteenths*.

Visual Clue: Swimming Pool

Use the image of a swimming pool as a mnemonic clue for converting fractions (see *Figure 9.12*). Students find it easier to convert fractions to decimals and improper fractions to mixed numbers with this visualization. When they need a decimal equivalent or to convert an improper fraction, students visualize or draw a swimming pool to the right of the fraction. The line between the numbers is visualized as a diving board. The number on the diving board (numerator) jumps into the swimming pool, setting up a division problem with the denominator as the divisor. Some students will also need to draw a division bracket in the swimming pool to complete the computation. Provide practice with the *Visual Clue: Swimming Pool* reproducibles on the CD.

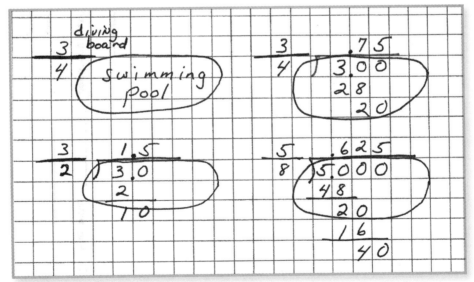

Figure 9.12: The swimming pool clue helps students remember how to convert fractions.

The Pattern of Eighths

Students who have difficulty with inversions find fractions confusing because as the numbers in the denominators increase, the value decreases. The pattern of eighths helps students understand and use *half*, *quarters*, and *eighths*. It enables students to put fractions back on the number line that they learned when they learned to count (in which each number is larger than the previous, as in *1, 2, 3, 4*, etc., instead of the opposite—where each fraction gets smaller—as in *1/2, 1/4, 1/8*). This allows students to compare the fractions *1/2* and *3/8* to determine which is larger (see *Figure 9.13*). Provide practice with *The Pattern of the Eighths* reproducibles on the CD.

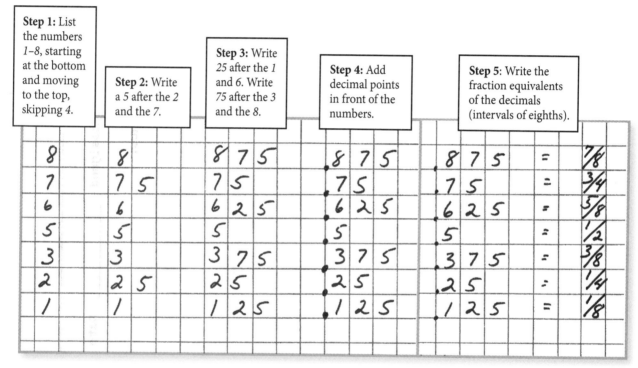

Figure 9.13: The pattern of eighths.

On a Personal Note:

Different Techniques for Different Learners

At one educational conference, I presented the pattern of eighths to a group of about 35 teachers. Many of them commented that they did not see how the pattern could help students. They said it would be easier for students just to learn how to convert fractions into decimals by dividing.

At the end of the session, after everyone else had left, a young teacher approached me and said, "You just released me from math prison." She said that ever since childhood, fractions and other math concepts were difficult for her to understand, and that the techniques I had demonstrated—especially the pattern of eighths—made more sense to her than anything else she had ever been taught. Even if you don't see the value of a specific technique, try it. It just may work.

The Pattern of Sixteenths

The pattern of sixteenths is developed from the pattern of eighths. Make sure students know how to produce the pattern of the eighths quickly and easily before attempting to teach the pattern of sixteenths.

Have students do the first three steps of the pattern of eighths, making sure there is space to write additional numbers between the listed numbers (see *Figure 9.14*). When students have completed this, they are ready to start the pattern of sixteenths. Have them write four pairs of *75* and *25* between the numbers of the patterns of eighths, as in the last column of *Figure 9.14*.

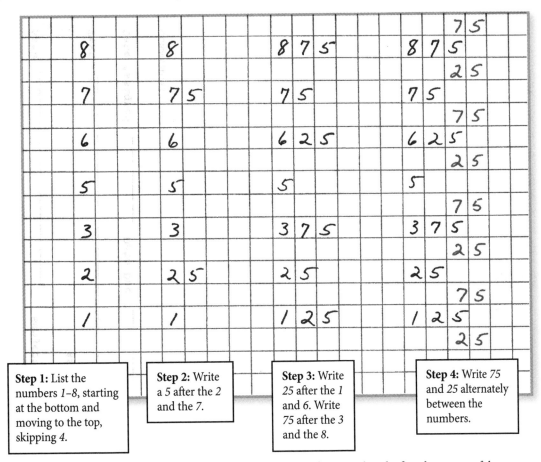

Step 1: List the numbers *1–8*, starting at the bottom and moving to the top, skipping *4*.

Step 2: Write a *5* after the *2* and the *7*.

Step 3: Write *25* after the *1* and *6*. Write *75* after the *3* and the *8*.

Step 4: Write *75* and *25* alternately between the numbers.

Figure 9.14: To use the pattern of sixteenths, students first complete the first three steps of the pattern of eighths and then write in pairs of 75 and 25.

Students then identify the odd eighths (*1/8, 3/8, 5/8, 7/8*) and the decimal equivalent of the eighths: *6, 8, 1,* and *3*. Working from bottom to top, they write the numbers, in order, in front of the pairs of *25* and *75* (as in *Figure 9.15*). Note that each number is used twice. Students then write in the numbers *0–9*, starting at the bottom and moving to the top, skipping *2* and *7* (see the second column in *Figure 9.15*). The pattern is complete when students write in decimal points before each number. If necessary, they also write out the equivalent fractions. Provide practice with *The Pattern of Sixteenths* reproducibles on the CD.

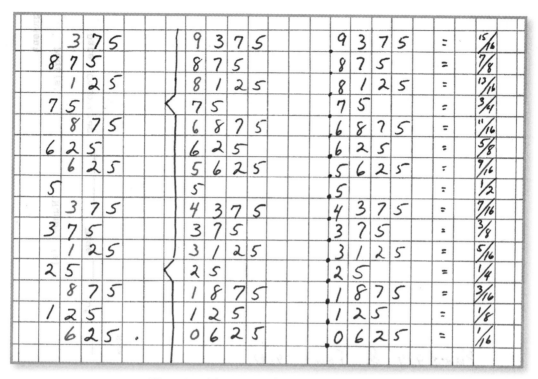

Figure 9.15: The pattern of sixteenths completed.

Decimals

Students usually do not have difficulty with decimal numbers that correspond to money. They know the numbers used with coins and bills because money is familiar and fascinating to them. But many students find decimal numbers that aren't used with money confusing. This may be due to a right/left discrimination problem that makes it difficult to deal with inversions (see Chapter 2, *Right/Left Discrimination*). Decimal numbers are inverse: They become larger as the quantities they represent become smaller. The following techniques will help you teach students how to read and work with decimals.

Graph paper. Use graph paper to help students keep their numbers and decimal points in line. For students with visual processing problems, it is better to use a whole block for the decimal point. Others can place the decimal point on the line between the blocks. See *Figure 9.16*.

Figure 9.16: Two ways to place the decimal point when using graph paper.

Money. Another way to help students work with decimals is to refer to money. A half-dollar is the same as *$0.50* and a quarter equals *$0.25*. Students can also reference money to understand the value of numbers that have more than two digits after the decimal point. Simply teach them to cover all but the first two digits to the right of the decimal point. This is also effective for teaching the differences between *.1* and *.01*. Show students how to box off all the numbers that are beyond the first two decimal places, as in *Figure 9.17*.

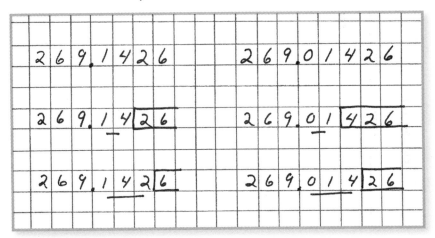

Figure 9.17: Students box off numbers in order to read decimals more easily.

Covering digits. Yet another way to use this technique is to have students place a finger over all but the first two digits after the decimal point. This enables students to compare numbers in order to better understand them. When students cover the rest of the digits, the visible number can be associated with money. Most students find money easy to understand because it is familiar and concrete.

When comparing *2.3586* to *2.03586*, students may think the second number is larger because it has more digits. When they cover everything except the two digits after the decimal point (see *Figure 9.18*), they can read the numbers as *$2.35* and *$2.03*. It's clear that the first number is larger.

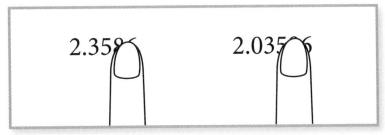

Figure 9.18: Covering the ending digits of decimals makes it easier to discern which number is larger.

When this skill is mastered, students can generalize the technique, using it to read larger decimals. They just move their finger to the right, comparing the hundredths, thousandths, and so on.

Decimal points first. Since students with visual tracking problems have difficulty lining up numbers and decimal points, it is often helpful to have them place the decimal points first when writing numbers, as in *Figure 9.19*.

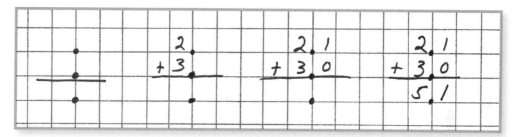

Figure 9.19: Students with visual challenges benefit by writing the numbers in after they write the decimal points.

The *OTH* pattern. When teaching students the place values to the right of the decimal point, use *OTH* (ones, tenths, hundredths) as a mnemonic clue (similar to the *HTO* pattern taught in Chapter 4, (*Place Value and Large Numbers*). Teach students to read the decimal point as the ones column (*O*). This makes it easier to remember that the number after the decimal point is in the tenths place.

When *HTO* and *OTH* are combined, it produces the mnemonic clue *OH TOOTH*, as in *Figure 9.20*. Tell students that one of the *O*s in the tooth has no value and can be extracted to help them remember that there is no ones-column after the decimal point.

Provide practice with the *Decimals* reproducibles on the CD.

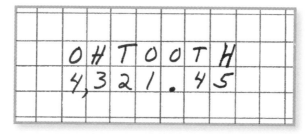

Figure 9.20: This mnemonic clue helps students read decimal numbers.

Percentages

Many students who have poor math skills understand percentages to some degree. They know if they get *60%* on an exam it is not as good as getting a grade of *90%*. They know that if something is on sale for *10%* off, it costs less than the marked price. But usually their understanding of percentages does not include much more than these basic concepts and so, as with fractions, they have difficulty completing calculations.

Students who have right/left discrimination problems often have difficulty learning how to calculate percentages because they cannot remember how to set up the calculation: "Do I divide the large number into the smaller one? Do I multiply or divide?" Even if students have learned to complete percentage computations in the past, they often have forgotten how to work with percentages. They do not know how to set up numbers for completing the computation, and they do not know how to check their answers.

Teach students how to convert percentages into decimals by moving the decimal point. Start by showing them how to determine *10%* by moving the decimal point one point place (see *Figure 9.21*). Next, teach students how to determine *1%* by moving the decimal point two places, as in *Figure 9.22*.

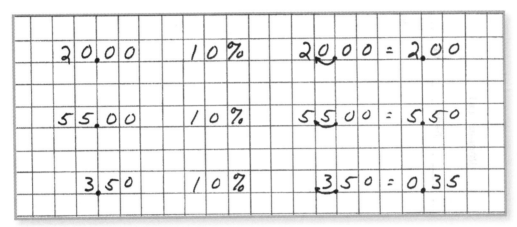

Figure 9.21: Teach students to move the decimal point to determine *10%*.

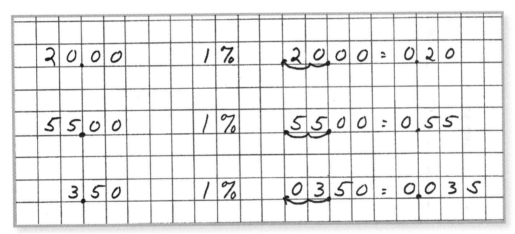

Figure 9.22: Determining *1%* by moving the decimal two places.

The next step uses the pattern of halves (see *Fractions* earlier in this chapter). Teach students to obtain *5%* by dividing *10%* in half, as in *Figure 9.23*. With these skills, students can determine the percentage of any number.

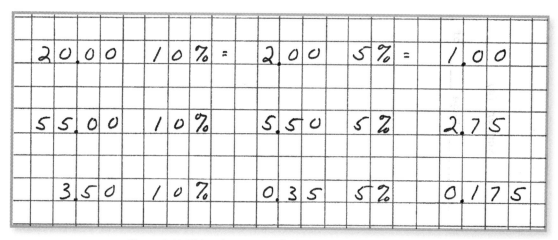

Figure 9.23: Using the pattern of halves to determine *5%*.

Then you can show students how to add together the numbers from *10%* and *5%* to determine *15%* of the whole (see *Figure 9.24*). When students have mastered determining *15%* in this way, the next step is to teach them how to determine and add in *1%*. This gives students the ability to find any percentage using addition.

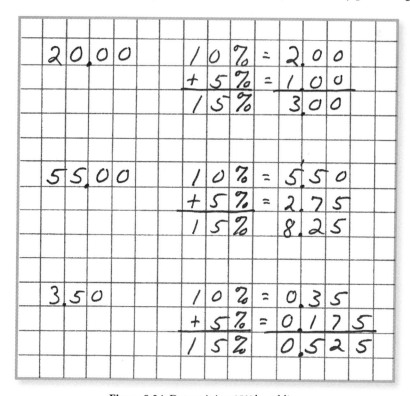

Figure 9.24: Determining *15%* by adding.

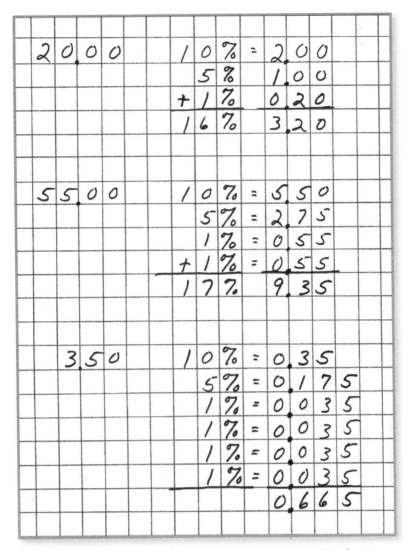

Figure 9.25: When students know how to determine *10%*, *5%*, and *1%*, they can determine any percentage by adding.

Although adding takes longer than other techniques, it is very useful for students who are just learning the concept of percentages or who need to see all the elements of the calculation. Provide practice with the *Percentages* reproducibles on the CD.

Conclusion

The ideas and techniques presented in this book are just a sampling of the many ways to teach math. This book is meant not as an end, but as a step in assisting all students to reach their fullest potential. The suggestions provided should help you when nothing else seems to be working and should serve as springboards for you.

There are many ways students struggle with math. Students may make frequent computation errors, have difficulty learning quantitative concepts, or have problems using math skills in daily life. Students are not born with an aversion to math, but some develop a dislike for the subject. Some even develop anxious responses to math. Students do not need to be diagnosed with a learning disability to struggle with math. Information gaps and insufficient or ineffective instruction lead to math problems. Students who are not diagnosed with a learning disability, but who perceive, process, and communicate differently, also have difficulties learning and remembering math.

You can help students who learn differently by using the techniques in this book to remediate, adapt, and accommodate. Students may also require alternative techniques to learn or relearn math concepts and operations or adapted instructional materials and tests. Those with significant disabilities may need formal accommodations.

Many students can move from needing adaptations and formal accommodations to mastery of concepts and techniques, but this is not possible for all. Never assume that a student who has a disability is unable to master the concepts and operations of math. But don't view students who continue to need adaptations and accommodations as failures either.

Sometimes students just don't seem to be able to understand a specific concept, and consequently this information remains as a gap in their knowledge. Understanding why gaps exist is the first step in helping students grasp basic math concepts. The second step is using the instructional techniques and activities in this book to reach students who are struggling.

Students who struggle with math often have difficulty with some of the most basic operations. The hierarchy of number-fact skills (see Chapter 3) provides a framework to work from. The techniques in Chapter 5 for teaching addition are often especially helpful. Students who have difficulty with addition tend to struggle with all math operations, so it's important to address these specific difficulties first.

Subtraction, multiplication, and division come easier to students if they have strong addition skills. When problems arise in these areas, try alternative ways of presenting concepts and experiment with new ways of teaching the operations. Some techniques are more complicated and involve many extra steps than the traditional ways of completing these operations, but for students who just do not seem to learn using the traditional ways, these techniques often work.

When first learning about fractions, students may easily grasp the concept of parts, but when numbers are used to represent these parts they become confused. Some students struggle with fractions, decimals, and percentages throughout their schooling. The techniques offered in Chapter 9 can supplement how you teach all your students and are especially useful to students who think and learn differently. You may never encounter students who need the extreme alternative techniques of the pattern of eighths or the pattern of sixteenths, but for the right student, they work wonders. They are included to provide as many ways as possible to help students.

This book is not a comprehensive guide for teaching students who have underdeveloped math skills. It is a collection of the techniques that I have found most helpful and effective with my students, of all ages. I developed many of the original ideas and techniques to match the thought processes of individuals rather than to match age- or grade-levels.

On a Personal Note:

Learning Differently

This affirmation helps my students. It may also help your students:

I might learn differently, but I learn well.

I have my students apply stickers of this affirmation to their notebooks. I have them repeat it every time we meet and whenever they get frustrated learning. I talk to them about what it means to learn differently and help them understand their strengths and weaknesses. As students come to understand their differences and accept them, they take the affirmation to heart. And when students do not understand what is being taught, they sometimes have the courage and assertiveness to say, "I do not understand because I learn differently. Could you please explain it a different way?" Gradually, as their math skills improve, students come to believe the affirmation.

Bibliography

Cooper, Richard. *Learning Differences, Problems, and Differences: Selected Topics.* Bryn Mawr, PA: Learning disAbilities Resources, 3rd Edition, 1999.

Cooper, Richard. *Teaching Math Instructional Guide.* Bryn Mawr, PA: Learning disAbilities Resources, 1996.

Gersten, Russell, and David Chard, "Number Sense: Rethinking Arithmetic Instruction for Students with Mathematical Disabilities," *The Journal of Special Education* 44 (1999): 18–28.

Osher, David, and Lenore Webb. *Adult Literacy, LD, and Social Context: Conceptual Foundation for a Learner-Centered Approach.* Washington, DC: U.S. Department of Education, Office of Vocational and Adult Education, February, 1994.

Pisaneschi, Patricia Y. "Using Tic-Tac-Toe Math: A Case Study," *PAACE Journal of Lifelong Learning* 10 (2001): 62–69.

Peterson Miller, Susan, and Cecil D. Mercer. "Educational Aspects of Mathematics Disabilities," *Journal of Learning Disabilities* 30, no. 1 (January–February 1997): 47–56.